AFRICA'S WILD LIFE

Survival or Extinction?

Scale of Miles
0   100   200   300   400   500

S U D A N   E T H I O P I A

UGANDA
11
EQUATOR
Kampala
12
PARC
NATIONAL ALBERT
KIVU
10
RUANDA
URUNDI

K E N Y A
2
Lake
Victoria
6 3
5 4
NAIROBI
16
15   13
14

1
8 7
9

Mombasa

C O N G O

Albertville   T A N G A N Y I K A

Lake Tanganyika

Dar es
Salaam

K A T A N G A

Elisabethville

N

N O R T H E R N
R H O D E S I A

Lusaka

Lake Nyasa

NYASALAND

M O Z A M B I Q U E

I N D I A N
O C E A N

Salisbury

S O U T H E R N
R H O D E S I A

Beira

Bulawayo

B E C H U A N A L A N D

SOUTH-WEST AFRICA

TRANSVAAL

Lourenço
Marques

Johannesburg

SWAZILAND

S O U T H   A F R I C A

BASUTOLAND

Durban

CAPE TOWN

East London
Port Elizabeth

KEY

KENYA:
1. Amboseli
2. Eldoret
3. Gatundu
4. Masai Reserve, Kajiado
5. Nairobi National Park
6. Naivasha (part of Aberdare National Park)
7. Tsavo East Royal National Park
8. Tsavo West Royal National Park
9. Voi (township)

UGANDA:
10. Queen Elisabeth National Park
11. Murchison National Park
12. Kasese

TANGANYIKA:
13. Arusha
14. Manyara National Park
15. Ngorongoro Crater
16. Serengeti National Park

NATIONAL PARKS AND RESERVES VISITED BY THE AUTHOR

DELETED

AFRICA'S WILD LIFE

Survival or Extinction?

———

ERIC ROBINS

WITH A FOREWORD BY
H.R.H. PRINCE BERNHARD
OF THE NETHERLANDS,
PRESIDENT OF THE WORLD WILDLIFE FUND

ODHAMS PRESS LIMITED
LONG ACRE · LONDON

First published 1963

TO BRIGITTE

MADE AND PRINTED IN GREAT BRITAIN BY
COX AND WYMAN LTD.,
LONDON, FAKENHAM AND READING
T.1262.NQ

CONTENTS

CONTENTS

ACKNOWLEDGMENTS

My warm and sincere thanks to those who assisted me in writing this book, in particular the proprietors of *Life* magazine who made the majority of my trips possible; their photographer Loomis Dean, tough, temperamental and talented, who made them doubly memorable; every individual dedicated to the protection and reprieve of Africa's wild animals; Miss Valerie Hefferon; Mrs. Barbara Vandewaal; Mr. Peter Hawthorne; Mr. Peter Mackay and other friends and colleagues, although they are synonomous, who willingly or unwittingly played their part in my exacting, but highly rewarding, task.

The Author.

ILLUSTRATIONS

MAPS

PLATES

7

ILLUSTRATIONS

PREFACE

By A. D. FRASER

*Director of Wild Life Conservation, Southern Rhodesia,
who planned and directed the daring rescues of wild animals
from the rising waters of Lake Kariba.*

THE Continent of Africa is restless and uneasy under the dazzling glare of the world spotlight. New States are emerging. Superimposed cultures and traditions are being discarded, and are being replaced. Now, as perhaps never before, is the face of Africa being changed, but whether for better or for worse only time will tell.

In this vast land mass there still exists today that priceless heritage of wild fauna and flora which belongs to Africa alone. Will these wild animals and their, as yet, unspoilt habitats, which are one of Africa's greatest natural resources and the envy of others, emerge from the turbulence unscathed to bring wealth and enjoyment to the human race in the years ahead? Can it be honestly said that the statesmen, the politicians and the peoples of Africa have even a vague notion of their responsibilities to mankind or to themselves in the preservation of these things that are of inestimable value?

From happenings over the last few years it has become apparent that various international and national agencies and bodies have become alarmed at the rate of disappearance of Africa's wild life, and have sensed the danger of it disappearing altogether.

Inspired by the desire to seek the facts, Eric Robins has conducted a searching investigation, the results of which are honestly portrayed in *Africa's Wild Life*. The inspiration is there, the warning is given; ignorance of the facts can no longer be claimed.

This particular book embraces many territories and many peoples and reveals, for the first time, the overall inside story of the plight of African wild life. If Eric Robins, through his efforts,

9

can stimulate interest and create an awareness, both in Africa and abroad, which results in some positive and worth-while action being taken to preserve and conserve the wild fauna and flora of the African Continent for the benefit and enjoyment of future generations, then he will have achieved his objective.

FOREWORD

By H.R.H. PRINCE BERNHARD
OF THE NETHERLANDS
President of the World Wildlife Fund

THERE are many people who still believe that the
vast continent of Africa is teeming with wild life.
Alas, this is not so, and unless vigorous efforts are
made within the next decade, it may well be that
our children's grandchildren will ask, "What was a
giraffe?" or what was a lion?"

Africa is a country in which I have had the opportunity to see first hand some of the problems with
which it is faced, and Mr. Robins, in this excellent
book, has thrown a dramatic spotlight with words
and pictures on the urgent need to save the wild life
of Africa.

INTRODUCTION

THE PROBLEM IN OUTLINE

IN order to understand the many factors affecting the game
animals of Africa it is useful to bear in mind that the degree of
control which can be exercised in any area depends on the legal
status of the land, the nature of the control specified and the zeal or
lack of it with which the authority controlling the area acts.

The author studied lands under the suzerainty of the Congo
(both Kivu Province and Katanga), Uganda, Kenya, Tanganyika,
Mozambique, Northern Rhodesia, Southern Rhodesia, the
Republic of South Africa and Ethiopia. The scope of game laws
varied considerably and so did the efficiency with which they were
applied. Four different terms to designate areas in which control of
game is planned are in fairly general use: National Park, National
Reserve, Game Reserve and Controlled Area. The following
details, though not precisely applicable in all areas, are taken from
the Sessional Paper No. 1 of 1959–60 of the Colony and Protectorate of Kenya, in which a majority of these areas are situated; they
give some idea of the manner in which enlightened Government
policy is intended to be put into operation. As will be observed
they also indicate some of the greatest difficulties which stand in
the path of effective implementation of a policy of game
preservation.

The declared policy of the Government of Kenya is "to preserve game to the greatest extent possible, having regard to human
interests and financial priorities". The effects of these two limitations are very great indeed.

The Trustees of the Royal National Parks are recognized by the
Government. However, the Government does not accept responsibility for the activities of game animals (it would be indeed a bold
man or body that was prepared to do so) and no compensation is

13

payable for damage caused by them. This cannot but influence the outlook of farmers, whether European or African, whose crops or cattle pastures are threatened with damage by wild animals. Yet the Government looks to the Trustees of the Royal National Parks to provide the main bastion in its long-term policy of game preservation.

Turning to the four different types of administrative control of areas mentioned above we will deal first with the NATIONAL PARK. Only if the overriding interests of the game in it will not run counter to human interests can an area be designated a National Park, and in a park game preservation and management have precedence over other interests. As such an area falls under the administration of a public body, the Trustees of the Royal National Parks, a permanent but very small force of wardens is maintained; available finance is the limiting factor. This permanent force at times receives help from volunteers who act as Honorary Game Wardens; without their assistance the plight of fauna in some districts would be more parlous than in fact it is. There is little glamour and much hard work for these valuable helpers.

In some areas seasonal migration of animals across the borders of National Park areas presents a special problem since the migration takes the animals into areas close to the Park boundaries where poaching is rendered easier by lack of adequate control. (District Commissioners and the Police do what they can, but manpower, sufficient completely to check depredations, simply is not available.)

NATIONAL RESERVES are areas in which the Trustees of the Royal National Parks were given complete or partial control but had to take cognizance of legitimate human rights. Though at first sight this difference from conditions in a National Park appears small, in fact it is fundamental. Particularly where the resident Africans have felt the pastures of their cattle to be threatened by game herds there has been trouble. Often widespread and indiscriminate killing of game animals has occurred. This has proved extremely hard to check because the areas are vast, the number of game rangers small and their equipment often comparatively antiquated. (Helicopters which could have greatly extended the range of effective patrols are few and lack of finance prevents any increase in their use.) Moreover, in many instances the sympathies of the resident Africans have been on the side of the killers of the game so that information has been forthcoming only with reluctance and the chance of effective prosecution has been very slim indeed. In consequence the National Reserves have proved largely a failure and are being abandoned.

A GAME RESERVE is an area controlled by the Game Department in which the hunting or capture of animals normally is prohibited. In special cases, however, the Chief Game Warden can authorize either killing or capture. Increasing effort is being directed to the encouragement of participation by African tribesmen in the protection of the Game Reserves, but it is no easy task to convince them that wild animals are a unique asset and indeed a possession of value to themselves. Yet the future of game in Africa will depend largely on the attitude of people towards it; therefore the Government is committed to the encouragement of measures designed to educate public opinion on the importance of game preservation, but funds available to support that policy are very small.

A CONTROLLED AREA is a region into which entry is restricted to persons who have been issued with permits, which are at the discretion of the Chief Game Warden who can attach any conditions or restrictions which he may think fit. Thus some parts of the region can be visited only by photographers while in other parts of it hunting may be allowed. In such parts the volume of hunting and the species of animals which may be hunted can in theory be controlled.

In the Controlled Area, as elsewhere, the limit placed by finance on the personnel available to enforce control means in practice there are not enough wardens to prevent poaching. Particular difficulty may be encountered when the poachers cross a national border before engaging in depredations. It would be unwise to be too sanguine about the prospects of African District Council Game Reserves and other locally sponsored enterprises since in all areas there are legitimate and apparently conflicting human interests. Even where the Africans derive profit from the sale of permits to photograph and hunt game and from the sale of meat resulting from the controlled culling of the game animals, it may take time to convince all that indiscriminate killing is not in their interests—and time is not on the side of preservation. Though some African District Councils are creating Game Reserves in the areas under their control—a move which undoubtedly should help in the preservation of game—there remain to be tackled the problems created by the annual grass fires which are lit by the Africans in the belief that they will improve the grazing for their flocks of sheep and goats. These fires are pushing their way farther into the tsetse country and present a great threat to wild life because they are rapidly destroying the thickets and riverside vegetation essential to some species such as buffalo, rhinoceros and lion.

Not all the governments exercising authority in East Africa are as alive to the importance of the problem of game preservation as could be desired; even where a government's intentions are of the best, the difficulties resulting from a clash of interests between the game animals and domestic cattle and also the depredations of poachers, concerned merely with the quick profit to be made from such items as elephant tusks or rhinoceros horn, are of such proportions that slaughter of animals continues at a far higher rate than will permit of their continued existence. It is against that background that the story unfolded in the following pages must be considered.

SECTION ONE

*

Kenya

During August, September and October, 1961, the author visited the Amboseli Reserve; Eldoret; Gatundu; the Masai Reserve; Nairobi Royal National Park; the Royal National Parks Tsavo East and Tsavo West and Voi.

In the chapters devoted to this area he tells of drought and the efforts to combat it by animals and man; of trade in ivory both legal and illicit; of the Masai, their customs and changing outlook; of Alexander Douglas and the giraffe herd he runs on his ranch; of the imagined properties of rhino horn which threaten the extinction of the animals and of the efforts being made with the help of modern drugs to preserve them.

B

NATIONAL PARKS AND RESERVES
IN KENYA AND TANGANYIKA

Chapter 1

LIVE AND LET LIVE

KENYA'S Amboseli Reserve, dominated by the plum-pudding and brandy-sauce mountain of Kilimanjaro, which is the highest and most impressive in Africa, is a dust-bowl of brilliance and beauty, of panoramic, shimmering mirages, of sandstorms thicker than London's pea-souper fogs—and the scene of overwhelming drama and death.

Amboseli is mainly flat country, consisting of lava ash thrown out by prehistoric volcanic activity. According to a single-sheet pamphlet for which, under the circumstances, we were glad to pay the 50 Kenya cents demanded to aid the Reserve, Amboseli takes its name from the dry lake bed some seven miles to the west of the Safari Lodge. Only in seasons of heavy rain does the lake contain any surface water.

"In dry weather it is smooth enough for cars to drive across it, and the extraordinary feature of such a journey is that the heat haze rising from the lake forms a remarkable mirage. Like all mirages it recedes as the observer approaches, making the whole scene most deceptive and sometimes dangerous as it is almost impossible to distinguish between the mirage and the actual surface water.... The mountain is often clear of cloud in the early mornings and late afternoon, and in certain seasons it stands out glistening in all its glory throughout an entire day.... Bird life at Amboseli is extremely varied, as it is on the migrational route of many non-resident birds and it also attracts many species which live near water. In the dry areas the ostrich stands supreme as the largest of all birds, and many of his smaller relations seem to find adequate food on the lava plains. Bustards, secretary birds, storks, hornbills, guinea fowl, francolins, and suchlike, abound in great numbers. Along the swamps one frequently sees a wide selection

19

of duck, egrets, jacanas (lily trotters) and other birds that find their food in or near water. Weavers, queleas, shrikes and woodpeckers, rollers, louries and long-toed plover add colour to the scene, and bird watchers will never have a dull moment."

A ceremony which marked the formal handing over in 1961 of the National Reserve to the Masai was held under a tall, yellow-stemmed thorn tree on the verge of Ol Tukai Safari Lodge. Amboseli had then been under the care of the trustees of the Royal National Parks of Kenya since 1948.

The Governor of Kenya, Sir Patrick Renison, told the Masai at the ceremony that they were doing more than just taking over a thriving concern.

"It is a kind of trust, since the world at large as well as the people of Kenya will anxiously watch the future management and progress of Amboseli." He added: "I feel sure that you are aware of this great responsibility and that you are willing and able to follow the splendid example which the trustees and their officers have shown you.

"I must, however, sound a word of warning. Amboseli's world renown is based on two main assets—its game and the splendour of this mountain, Kilimanjaro. Of its game the rhinos are, perhaps, the most important because of their tameness and willingness to be photographed. But there is a danger that one of those assets, the rhinos, may disappear. I have been informed that this year very many of them have been illegally killed for their horns. If these rhinos disappeared entirely, Amboseli would lose much of its attraction for tourists. Each animal, therefore, is worth many thousands of shillings to you and your Council if it remains alive. But dead it is worth only a few shillings to the selfish and miserable poachers who killed it. I hope therefore that you will take the sternest measures to prevent and stamp out this illegal theft of your assets."

The Vice-Chairman of the Kajiado African District Council, young and handsome Mr. Jason Ole Sein, expressed the gratitude of the Masai people for the move whereby they could derive a greater financial benefit from the game "which we have always lived alongside in our district, sharing our grazing and our watering points, although the game has sometimes reacted unkindly in stealing the occasional cow or goat".

The Masai were grateful for the opportunity not only to benefit financially but to show that they had always adopted the policy of "live and let live" so far as game was concerned.

Mr. Ole Sein went on: "We mean to continue this policy and even, if possible, improve on it. We can see that in game and tourism we have a valuable addition to our district revenue and in a year, such as this, when so many of our cattle have died and when famine is abroad and when we are in desperate need of revenue for our day-to-day expenses, we appreciate every cent we can obtain."

Mr. Sein pointed out that the Masai were a cattle-herding people and could not live entirely on the proceeds of tourism. They wanted to leave suitable areas for game, but to develop other areas as ranches.

"It is important," he continued, "that we provide grazing and water for our people in suitable areas so that we can begin to show them that they should settle down in family groups instead of the nomadic life they now follow which brings disaster in times of drought. Only, too, in this way can we educate our people to care for the land and prevent large-scale erosion."

It would be one of the first aims of the Masai, he said, to put permanent roads in the Amboseli area as the present dusty tracks were scarcely tolerable to the vegetation, the game and, most important, the paying visitors. They would have to train their young men to run Amboseli. They wanted educated Masai youth, too, to go on for further education in the branches of science which made a study of flora and fauna.

"All this needs cash, and our coffers have been sadly depleted by drought," he said. "We hope the Government will keep this very much in mind as only a satisfied, prosperous people will happily and whole-heartedly care for the game which is so important for attracting foreign visitors. We want to help with game. We need the Government's help for ourselves, and then we can all live happily together."

There were brave and inspiring words on both sides that day. Long after the printer's ink on them had dried and their broadcast echoes had faded, I paid my first visit to arid and magnificent Amboseli.

It was there that I met the most photographed wild beast in the world—"Gertie" the rhino with the heart of gold. She was lying peacefully in a dust wallow with her latest calf. On her grey hide perched a tick bird, snapping up insects. The birds also give a warning of approaching danger to these short-sighted animals.

"Gertie" was born before the last world war and she was known among the tribesmen as "Koormi" or "the one with the long nose". The title was well earned, for "Gertie" when adult carried an incredible 54¼-in.-long front horn which broke all records in her domain. When I encountered her—normally as tame as any domestic cat—love had robbed her of her glory. Her horn was then undoubtedly the shortest in the rhino world.

"Lovely old girl," said the Ambolesi warden, grizzled, bush-wizard Major W. H. M. "Tabs" Taberer, affectionately. "A real star too." (See facing page 120.)

This rhino has featured in several films, and had her photograph many times in newspapers in every country. In 1955, after her rival "Gladys" had lost 18 in. off the tip of her horn, "Gertie" became the most sought after animal in the Amboseli.

Her romantic and fascinating history is told by "Tabs" Taberer in a report to the Kenya Wild Life Society.

"Almost every visitor to Ol Tukai Lodge has, on arrival, inquired her whereabouts and would depart with a happy sense of having seen her or captured her picture or, perhaps, with a feeling that the trip was not quite complete as 'Gertie' was in a mood and would not show herself. With all this attention 'Gertie' became so tame that she would lie in a dust bath with her off-spring and allow several cars at a time to approach within thirty feet, and not bother to get up and often just continue to sleep. There have been some incidents: when she refused to move some unkind visitor, wanting action in his pictures may deliberately drive his vehicle at her and on such occasions she will take her calf off into the bush to sulk for several days and not be seen. Such behaviour is as good as a report to us that there is, or has been, a hooligan in the area who has disturbed her as she seldom otherwise hides herself except when calving or mating."

Major Taberer first saw "Gertie" in 1947. He recalls that she was then living around Ol Toroto waterholes, in the vicinity of Kitirua, some seven miles from her present habitat. She was running with a two-and-a-half-year-old calf at the time. So she was most aggressive and practically unapproachable in a vehicle. She would either charge on sight or disappear. "Gladys", too, was in the same area and the two would often be together. As the wells in the outlying areas began to dry up more and more Masai brought their cattle up to the much needed waters of Kitirua. So the two female rhino, with a number of companions, moved away to take up their present headquarters in the area of Observation Hill. There they came in frequent contact with motor cars and human noises.

"At first they were very shy and nervous and would either charge or hide," said Major Taberer. "But after a couple of years they settled down, realizing that the noisy monsters on four wheels presented no danger. It was in 1953 that 'Gertie' settled in at her new home, bringing with her a newly-born bull calf. This little oddity had only half a tail, and no ears at all. He soon received the name of 'Pixie'. The two presented a rare sight. The mother with incredibly long horn and the curious little son with just two holes where the ears should be. They were the real showpiece of Amboseli and, as a result, took longer to settle down as a result of being so much in demand. However, once they realized there was nothing to fear, they became the tamest and most tolerant of all.

"There was great consternation when, at the end of April 1956, 'Gertie' suddenly disappeared, leaving behind a forlorn 'Pixie' who was then only three-and-a-half years old. 'Gladys' and family took the little chap over and allowed him to join them. However, only two weeks later, and amidst great relief and excitement, 'Gertie' suddenly re-appeared. She was seen proudly to display to a party of six others a tiny and timid but nevertheless complete female calf. 'Pixie' was allowed to join his wee sister and the three roamed together for two years."

On 17 March, 1958, "Gertie" mated with a bull strange to the area. The event was witnessed by a party of visitors and Taberer was able to keep a record of the date.

"'Gertie' and her calf had been seen at midday in a wallow. She was seen again at 4.30 that afternoon, then minus about a foot of her wonderful horn. Between these two times she went to the swamp for a drink, returning to the same wallow. Although we searched both ways along her tracks and for several days dug around the wallow with a tractor and by hand, we never found the tip. Although this was a great loss we had expected it to happen as the end was wearing very thin through dragging when she was feeding low. And no matter in what position she was lying the tip was always resting on the ground. Poor girl, she did look odd, but only four weeks later she was to look even odder.

"The swamp levels suddenly began to rise and spilled over to start the Semak River flowing again. This additional water attracted a number of new males to the area.

"In an encounter with one of these irascible gentlemen 'Gertie' lost the remainder of that beautiful front horn, which broke off right at the roots. This was indeed a major tragedy. She was seen a day after the battle bleeding profusely from the hole where the horn had been. The entire Ranger force started at once on a search. Tracking back, they came on the scene of battle and from there took up the hunt in earnest, eventually recovering the horn."

"Tabs" states that the unfortunate accident made not the slightest difference to "Gertie's" nature. She was as quiet and placid as ever.

"However, 'Gertie' was to have her reward and to hold her

Of the animals shown on this page the quagga (*top, right*) is extinct, the bontebok (*top, left*) and blesbok (*right*) nearly so. A reminder of how quickly this has come about is that those old enough to have enjoyed the writings of Rider Haggard and, more recently, John Buchan ("The blesbok are changing ground"), will recall that whole herds of these animals were common in the early years of this century. Of the white rhinoceros (*below, left*) and white-tailed gnu (*below, right*) there are few survivors outside zoos. How many of the world's wild animals will remain in their natural habitats in another decade depends on Man. . . .

Contrasts in the Ngorongoro Crater.

Above: A mixed herd of domesticated sheep and goats shepherded by a Masai boy. The animals keep close together for self-protection; in doing so they eat almost every blade of grass—so when they have passed the virtually naked soil is ripe for erosion. After that nothing grows. Then with their cattle facing starvation the Masai move them to denude more land.

Below: When wildebeest or any other type of grazing animals live together in large numbers in the wild they space themselves out so that the grass is not entirely consumed in one place. They also carefully avoid each other's droppings so that parasites are not transmitted from one animal to another. This picture shows part of a vast herd of wildebeest in the Ngorongoro Crater near the Seringati Reserve in northern Tanganyika.

Right: Travelling to and from the areas in which they graze, the cattle of African tribes usually are driven in long columns on a narrow front. As beast follows beast their hooves cut up the ground until it is broken and channeled; vegetation is entirely destroyed; then the hot sun makes dust and wind blows the soil away, so adding to the desolation resulting from over-cropping by the tightly packed grazing herds of the Masai.

There is a charm about the young of most animals that powerfully attracts most human beings—indeed who would not be tempted to try to play with the baby baboon (*left*) investigating the car mirror? Yet to do so would be to court danger—his parents (*below*) could not divine your intentions and might attack in his defence. Hence the rule that travellers in Africa's National Parks shall get out of vehicles only in approved places.

head even higher. On 13 July, about 2.30 p.m., she produced another little son exactly sixteen months after she had mated. This was a great event, and what a consolation prize for having become the ugliest rhino in the area, where she not so long ago was the proudest and most picturesque of them all. She has now produced five calves since I have known her, and I sincerely hope she will have a lot more."

The broken part of the horn recovered measured 39½ in. By projecting a side view of "Gertie" on to the screen and blowing the picture up to a size that fitted the piece exactly, "Tabs" has been able to measure the missing section as being 14¾ in.

"If these measurements are correct, and I do not believe they can be out, where did she stand with her 54¼ in. in the record list for a normal rhino horn. And where, in turn, was 'Gladys' whose horn was at one time several inches longer?" he asks.

In January, 1962, poachers claimed "Gladys". Four men speared her to death when patrols of game rangers were bogged down following heavy rains. The poachers hacked off what remained of her prize horn for sale to Asian or Arab traders. They also slashed off a flattened ear, a distinguishing feature, in a bid to hide her identity.

Enranged Masai guardians of Amboseli quickly brought the culprits to book. Each was sentenced to three years' imprisonment.

Chapter 2

BABOONS IN A SANDSTORM

WATCHED by groups of tourists and Masai tribesmen, six brown-uniformed African game rangers drawn up at the main gate of the lodge in Amboseli saluted smartly at a stacatto command from Sergeant Mwanzia Mutiaya. The doves in the trees cooed "uhuru". Kilimanjaro, with its deep snowline, stood out in majestic relief in the early morning sun.

Major Taberer introduced me to his guest, chain-smoking Major Ian Grimwood, head of Kenya's Game Department, and we talked of the drought and poaching as banks of grey cloud drifted towards the mountain. "Rain," said "Tabs" Taberer, "but not for us. There will be downpours on the other side of Kilimanjaro, right out of the Park. If only we could follow California's example and seed those clouds with rockets." He sighed: "But each rocket costs £150."

Major Grimwood estimated that the drought in Kenya and Tanganyika had killed off two-thirds of the emaciated Masai cattle.

"Tribal suicide," he interjected as "Tabs" remarked, "Perhaps they'll appreciate now there's no point in raising humps with four legs."

Despite his many burdens, Major Taberer was that day in a more cheerful and optimistic mood than a month after the July handing over of Amboseli to the Masai. When he took count of killings in the Park and swore in black despair that the only solution seemed to be to ship all the animals to South America and start all over again. At that time, apart from unconfirmed reports of five lions slaughtered, two elephant, five rhino and four giraffe had been speared to death by poachers and two buffalo calves had been fatally trampled down in a stampede of Masai cattle on a grazing ground normally reserved for game. The dead giraffe had been stripped of their hides for shields. The horns of four of the rhino had been removed. Zebra were being killed for their tails alone—to make fly-whisks.

"The African District Council supported me fully in my efforts to stamp out such wanton slaughter," Major Taberer told me. "The councillors were ready to hand out very rough justice. Two of them visited the Park and were horrified by the work of the poachers."

Touring Amboseli with "Tabs" and Major Grimwood, I saw spirals of smoke which guided us to a Masai village that had been set ablaze the day before when the tribesmen and their wives and families had moved on to the hills in search of grazing land. Three hundred head of cattle had died there from drought. Their skeletons, picked clean by the vultures and hyenas, were scattered in the volcanic dust. "Tabs", who had worked in Amboseli for over twelve years, said he hoped the Masai councillors would pass a law barring cattle from the Park area. The Masai would not kill their cattle even when the bulls, cows and calves were dying.

In the heart of the Amboseli "desert" there was a broad strip of rich green grass, a lengthy oasis marking the course of a spring which had burst out following earth tremors. A small river in the Park had been dammed by "Tabs" to flood the thirsty surrounding sandy soil and create patches of verdant grass for game grazing. Elsewhere he had directed the waters of river and swamps, which are fed by volcanic springs, into specially-cut channels to create cattle waterholes away from the game areas.

From the top of stumpy, rock-strewn Observation Hill we watched a 45-mile-an-hour sandstorm sweeping across the Park in an awesome yellow and red curtain which eclipsed the sun. Later on our journey we encountered a group of Masai boys and girls herding cattle through the haunts of lion, rhino and elephant. They were unarmed except for sticks, and the eldest appeared to be no more than twelve.

Two fully-grown elephants and a young bull were feeding in a weed-covered waterhole. That meant for them a change of diet. In Amboseli the elephants generally are forced to eat branches and leaves and in so doing they batter down more and more trees. This destroys trees faster than they grow and produces a vicious circle resulting in constantly lessening fodder for the elephants.

Emerging from the sandstorm which had set the baboons around us choking, we drove across the sun-baked lava bed of Amboseli Lake, passing the grotesque skeleton of a giraffe which "Tabs" believed to have been another victim of the drought. A mile away from the lake was the mirage of another. Unlike man, animals in search of water do not, according to Major Taberer, make their way towards mirages.

At dusk we came across a rarely-seen family group of six rhino in a dust wallow with red-billed ox-pickers on their backs. One of the group had no ears which, said Major Taberer, was a result of in-breeding. He took a lot of rousing, with "Tabs" brandishing his bush-hat frantically to make him charge the Land-Rover for pictures, but finally obliged. Our host then considerably quickened our interest by telling us that a charge by another rhino in the Park had once overturned a three-ton lorry!

There was a colourful, impromptu *indaba* next day which illustrated the Masai's possession of the Park. Guarded by two fierce, spear-toting warriors, a party of Masai elders arrived at the Lodge from up-country. After they had been welcomed by Major Taberer they sat in council under a thorn tree. Five African game rangers, who formed a guard of honour to one side on the perimeter of the Lodge, were curiously and closely inspected by the elders. The master of ceremonies was himself a Masai, 33-year-old Mr. Ambrose Moses Seney from Kajiado, who wore a new khaki bush-jacket and trousers as Acting Junior Assistant Warden of the Park.

Born in a tribal hut, mission-educated Mr. Seney came to Amboseli in 1954 to work as an assistant clerk in the Lodge office after passing the Kenya African Primary Examination. He was given his assistant warden's appointment, which could lead to him being in charge of the Park, at the time of the transfer to Masai administration. Based at the Lodge, he goes out regularly with the rangers on field work, including anti-poaching trips, and is also responsible for general administration, supervision of the sixty-three members of the African staff of the Lodge, and for dealing with tourist visitors of all colours and nationalities.

"My people must come to realize the great value of the game," he says. "The animals attract tourists from all parts of Africa and the world who put into the country large sums of money which benefit all the people, not only the Masai."

Ambrose Seney, gentle apostle of the African wild, is making a full and significant contribution towards that end.

Chapter 3

BOWL OF BLOOD

THERE is a charming African fable which tells how the white-haired Great Chief Le-eyo called his children around him to take leave of them after distributing his wealth.

Asked what he wanted the eldest son replied, "Something of everything upon the earth."

Le-eyo shook his head sadly. "Then take a few head of cattle, some goats and sheep and some of the food of the earth for there will be a large number of things," he said.

The younger son, however, asked only for a fan which the old man carried.

"My child, because you have chosen this fan God will give you wealth," his father replied. "You will be great amongst your brother's people."

The fable claims that the greedy elder son became a barbarian while his young brother, who spurned riches and material comforts, grew up to become the father of East Africa's noble and warlike Masai tribe.

On his walk from Mombasa to Lake Victoria in 1883, Joseph Thomson, the first white man to achieve such a feat and after whom the gazelles are named, found the Masai, much as they are today, a pastoral nomadic tribe living on milk and blood, and meat when available, while they grazed their flocks and herds over vast areas. At that time they dominated most of the other East African tribes, having standing armies of warriors drawn from the youthful age-grades, and operating with a skill, resource and bravery matched only by the fierce impis of the Zulus. Military service was then compulsory for all Masai youths between the ages of seventeen and thirty.

In 1911 the tribe in Kenya moved into a unified area of some

20,000 square miles and today its population is estimated at some 60,000 men, women and children. Before 1961's disastrous drought and floods in Kenya, it was estimated that the Kenya Masai owned about three-quarters of a million head of cattle. They all were thin, diseased and in poor condition, yet they represented the Masai's wealth which was counted by heads of cattle, not by their condition. The vast herds were creating grave over-grazing problems in the Masai reserve, particularly around the limited watering places, since much of the country is bone dry for long periods.

It has been frequently and truly stated that the Masai have much natural charm and inspire great affection in those with whom they come in contact. The Masai's ancient tribal laws decree that they shall not kill their cattle for meat but harmlessly draw off their blood for food.

At a tribal village in the hills fifteen miles from Kajiado, administrative centre of the Kenya reserve, we found a party of *Moran* (young warriors) preparing for the blood-letting ceremony against a background of low, box-shaped mud huts. Covered from head to foot with red mud mixed with ochre, their oiled, matted hair in pigtails and wearing sandals made from strips cut from truck tyres, the warriors—their leader chanting in a high-pitched falsetto—began exuberant war dances in our honour. They carried long metal spears and buffalo-hide shields, on which intricate patterns were painted in cattle blood, white powder of bleached bones and yellow soil. They broke their ranks individually to vie with each other in leaping stiffly high into the air while the women and village maidens, half naked, but wearing deep necklets of multi-coloured beads, watched ecstatically. Tottering picannins could not resist the temptation of joining in the dance.

The District Officer told us that the Masai and Kamba, traditional enemies, believe that a woman's urine is the best antidote to poisoned arrows. "I know of one man with a poison arrow in his arm after a clash with the Kamba, who recovered after a few mouthfuls," he said.

A beast was chosen from the village pen and led into a clearing.

As two of his companions gripped the cow and after a leather ligature had been tied around its neck in such a manner that the veins became swollen to make a clear target, a kneeling elder shot an arrow into the jugular of the animal from a distance of about three feet. The arrow head consisted of a characteristic thin steel tip about half an inch in length, set in a rubber hilt. The arrow was swiftly withdrawn and a *moran* darted forward with a gourd, or "kibuyu" to catch the thin fountain of blood flowing from the neck of the cow. After about a pint of blood had been taken from the animal, which did not appear to be in any acute pain or distress, the bleeding vein was smothered with mud and the beast allowed to go free.

With its calf standing by, another scraggy cow was milked by a woman of the village who, before handing over the milk to an elder to be mixed with the cattle blood, scattered a few drops on the ground as an offering to the tribal gods. Half of the newly drawn blood was poured into another gourd and vigorously stirred by a Masai grey-beard to congeal it.

Sugar, thorn tree leaves and secret medicinal herbs from the bush are often mixed with the blood, but rarely urine and cattle dung as is popularly believed.

A *moran*, wearing a streaming head-dress of black ostrich feathers, came forward and for our photographer gingerly sampled with a stick gobbets of the congealed blood from an enamel bowl. He went through his act with a distasteful reluctance which puzzled us until an elder explained that, contrary to custom, women had been present at the drawing off of blood and the young warrior felt that his meal might be bewitched or turned to poison.

The Masai women and girls crowded round in wonderment as Veterinary Officer Patrick Scoggins played back his tape recordings of them singing in unison with the village warriors. The *moran*, although equally intrigued, were too proud to join the women in the excited scramble to hear the recordings, but remained aloof, leaning on their spears and pretending that the white man's "magic box" held no wonders for them.

31

The village chief, courteous and dignified Kipopo Ole Loisa, approached me in his cloak of rock rabbit skins and raised his black staff, made from the heart of a thorntree, in greeting. The Chief is a leading member of the Masai African District Council at Kajiado which now controls Ambolesi Reserve.

"My people have been great hunters of the lion, the elephant, the rhino and other large animals," he said gravely. "They were our enemies. Today they are our friends. We now realize the value of preserving them because the money from tourists all over the world will help us to become good and useful citizens."

The chief added that, accordingly, he had forbidden his warriors to take part in any further traditional lion hunts in which the animal—one which has been raiding cattle is generally chosen—is attacked and killed with spears to blood the weapons and set the seal on a *moran*'s manhood.

Big strides have been made in recent years showing the Masai tribe the benefits of keeping fewer and better cattle and both men and women are becoming keen on educational facilities. Courses in agricultural husbandry were successfully started at Senya in the Kajiado district in a school situated in an old Mau Mau camp.

"The local African District Council has been searching for a way of educating the *moran* and interesting them in occupations other than cattle herding," genial Tom Edgar, District Commissioner at Kajiado, who founded the school, told me.

The drought had taken heavy toll of the Masai cattle and forced the young men to wander the country in search of food. When the school opened fifty Masai from various sections of the Reserve applied for admittance. One walked 125 miles to join.

"They are learning that the pen is mightier than the spear," added Mr. Edgar. "We are aiming to show them something of Western civilization and a little of the outside world to get them interested in following careers such as in the police or the army."

On arriving at the school the *moran* put away their spears, shields and knives and many cropped their shoulder-length hair in a symbolic gesture at the gateway to a new life.

Some idea of the vast areas the game rangers have to patrol can be gathered from this photograph taken when a Tiger Cub aeroplane was guiding a ranger patrol to poachers who had been spotted from it. It is unfortunate that limitations of finance prevent anything approaching an adequate use being made of either light aeroplanes or helicopters in anti-poaching measures.

Above: Game rangers of Kenya examining a poacher's arrowhead. From it they will be able to determine the tribe to which the hunters belong. One of the most destructive of the poachers' weapons is the poisoned arrow, silent in use, deadly in effect; the poison most commonly employed is a juice extracted from a small tree superficially resembling wild privit; the grove on the *left* is in Kenya. *Below:* A detachable spear head with a wire that makes it a land-type harpoon.

Some idea of the vast areas the game rangers have to patrol can be gathered from this photograph taken when a Tiger Cub aeroplane was guiding a ranger patrol to poachers who had been spotted from it. It is unfortunate that limitations of finance prevent anything approaching an adequate use being made of either light aeroplanes or helicopters in anti-poaching measures.

Above: Game rangers of Kenya examining a poacher's arrowhead. From it they will be able to determine the tribe to which the hunters belong. One of the most destructive of the poachers' weapons is the poisoned arrow, silent in use, deadly in effect; the poison most commonly employed is a juice extracted from a small tree superficially resembling wild privit; the grove on the *left* is in Kenya. *Below:* A detachable spear head with a wire that makes it a land-type harpoon.

Mr. Edgar confirmed that an increasing number of Masai chiefs were taking the lead, on their own initiative, in game conservation. He was convinced that the handing over of Amboseli to the Masai was helping to save East Africa's wild game.

"The Masai kill animals which they think are menacing their cattle herds," he said, "but I feel the slaughter of big game by them would have been double in recent times without the Amboseli move."

Chapter 4

ANIMAL GRAVEYARD

"CHEERS," said wiry, little Ian Parker of the Kenya Game Department. He had come to Voi to give evidence against a rhino poacher and, after the case, we were having a lunch-time beer in the lounge of the hotel. It was a welcome break from his normal job of cropping elephant by shooting in an area outside Tsavo Royal National Park, cutting up the carcasses and drying the meat for sale to Africans. The ears are disposed of for an average of £2 each to make shoes and handbags.

During our chat, Ian mentioned casually that twenty miles from the town there was a dead elephant which had been struck by a passenger express on the main Nairobi–Mombasa railway while fleeing from poachers towards the safety of the Park. Elephants on railway lines are increasingly rare sights in Africa so I jumped into a Land-Rover to follow Ian's careering truck to the spot. The victim, a young male, lay by the side of the rails, a mountain of grey flesh guarded by a group of tribesmen who had found the body and were waiting for their rewards in the shape of cuts of meat.

"It's amazing how some animals know they will be safe in the parks," said Ian. "They will cross from open hunting areas into game reserves and just stand there flaunting their freedom."

The dead elephant's ears and the tusks, which were later sold by auction for £30, were hacked off with pangas and axes by Parker's black game scouts and loaded into the truck with thick cutlets of the trunk, a delicacy which they claimed as their right.

At a nod from Ian, the tribesmen went to work, slashing up the body while their wives and children stood by with enamel bowls in which to carry off the meat on their heads. One exuberant elder, bathed in blood, crawled into the beast's stomach and peered out from among the entrails. Trains passed by unheeded as the tribesmen chanted happily, "Uhuru Na Kenyatta, Uhuru Na Ndofu"—"Freedom and Kenyatta, Freedom and Elephant"— until little but a tall cage of bones was left for the vultures and kites.

*   *   *

I returned to Voi to meet the legendary David Sheldrick at his headquarters there. These were the formal biographical details I had been given of the man by his superiors in Nairobi; "He was born in Kenya in November, 1919, and was educated at a school in Britain. After spending some time as a farmer, he joined the glamorous team of professional hunters and earned for himself a good reputation as a keen hunter, able tracker and a first-class shot. The war then intervened during which he served with the K.A.R. in the Middle East and Burma, retiring with the rank of major. Soon after the war, he decided to abandon the pursuit of professional hunting and joined the National Parks service in 1949, going to the Tsavo Royal National Park where he has been ever since. During the Mau Mau Emergency he rendered valuable service with tracker teams and in hunting down terrorists as a member of the Kenya Police Reserve. He subsequently returned to the Tsavo Park where he organized, and successfully concluded, a campaign against the poachers in recognition of which, and of other services, he was appointed a Member of the Order of the British Empire. He is an accepted authority on poaching and elephants."

David is Warden in charge of the eastern section of Tsavo Royal National Park. This Mau Mau rebellion hero and fabulous white hunter turned game warden is as handsome as any matinée idol, and to strangers appears faintly arrogant in a typically British way in his devotion to his work.

He was coldly angry when I arrived. For at his feet, in hand-cuffs, squatted a puny, phlegmatic rhino poacher surrounded by his bow and poisoned arrows, gourd, metal cook-pot, and a blood-stained, fibrous rhino horn.

"He'll probably go to prison for a good long term," muttered David, smoothing down his immaculate bush-shorts. "But that means nothing, except regular meals for once and a roof over his head. These chaps still call gaol 'King George's Hotel'."

He walked off back to his office, leaving the poacher to the African guards and his fate.

In a wooden cage near his house at Voi David Sheldrick had a young lioness which he had found on the plain, weak from hunger. A porcupine quill in her nose had prevented her from eating. I watched the lioness being fed on a diet of raw meat and glucose before being trucked to Nairobi to be released in the Royal National Park there. In a pen close by was an affectionate baby rhino rescued from the bush a few weeks before after its parents had died of starvation in the worst drought in the history of Tsavo East. It shared the pen with three buffalo orphans, all thriving on bales of dried lucerne. They were happy and contented in the hands of man, safe from the grim and stark reality of the ravaged wilds into which David took us that morning.

It was a dusty, fifty-mile ride through a Valley of the Doomed. Everywhere was arid, sandy soil. On the "battlefields" of dead, dying and smashed down trees the bitter-sweet stench of putrefaction pervaded.

Hungry rhino and their calves were seen desperately searching for food among gaunt, dust-whitened trees on the skyline of this 4,000-square-mile Animal Graveyard.

As we pitched our tents by the sluggishly-flowing Athi River, an elephant herd, which had trekked some thirty miles across the dead land to drink, wandered off in line ahead and a male rhino, its flanks bearing the broad, black patches of malnutrition, the fatal stigmata, staggered through the tinder-dry brushwood.

"They are dying at the rate of two and three a day," said Sheldrick. "Tsavo once had Africa's biggest concentration of rhino, but they may soon be as extinct as the dodo."

African game rangers called to him from the bush. They had found the emaciated body of a newly-dead female rhino, and 300 yards away was another rhino drought victim lying in a pit of sand created by its death agonies. We moved on to find the hyena-torn carcass of a baby elephant which had dropped dead of hunger and exhaustion after crossing the parched terrain with a herd making for the river.

"When they go down, they stay down," said Sheldrick brokenly.

No vultures wheeled in the cloudless sky. "There are too many dead for the vultures to need to fly in search of prey," he added.

We found three more dead rhino that afternoon within a radius of three miles. One, still alive, was trapped between two tree stumps, its head hanging a few feet above the river. Pretty Mrs. Sheldrick soaked her cardigan in the river and sprinkled the stricken animal's snout with water in an effort to revive it. It died seconds later with a convulsive shudder.

"Heart breaking," she said tearfully. "For years my husband has been trying to stop people killing these creatures—and now all this."

There was a rustle in the undergrowth and, as David strolled towards the spot, a young rhino burst into view and charged straight at him. He dodged quickly aside and his game rangers fell on the squealing, terrified animal, throwing it expertly like a steer. Its left hind leg had been badly mauled by a lion. With a glance, Sheldrick assessed the tragedy. The calf, lying beside the body of its dead, starved mother, had been attacked by a lion, but had managed to escape despite its injuries.

From his bush-kit Sheldrick took out a hypodermic which he filled with a tranquillizer and gave her two shots in the flank as the Africans continued to wrestle with her. At the first bid Sheldrick bent the long, tough needle in half on the armour-plated hide. Soon, however, the rhino was inert. It was lifted bodily into the truck by a dozen Africans and taken off to the river camp. Given grass, dried milk and shots of penicillin, it lay in the stockade of branches and thorn bushes. After several attempts to break out, as lions roared and growled along the river bank, the rhino died during the night from the shock of its capture, exhaustion and the effects of its wounds.

With the stunted bushes on which rhino feed cropped bare all around, Sheldrick, his bush radio-telephone crackling, decided to mount a simple mercy operation of beating Nature in the hope of saving these animals.

Working an average of twelve to fourteen hours a day, which, like most wardens in East Africa, he considered normal, Sheldrick, set up quick-linking sections of light metal pipeline, to pump water at 8,000 gallons an hour, 200 yards from the River Athi to a seven-foot tall sprinkler standing among the brown bushes. The circling 150-ft. jet of artificial rain from the sprinkler created a rainbow of hope in the morning sun, the dry earth gave up a smell of ambrosia, and birds circled overhead in wonderment as David offered a silent prayer that the bushes would be brought to leaf within a few days. It was a vivid illustration of the maxim that water is more precious than gold in Africa.

As we prepared to set off to the dried-up Tiva River in another section of the Park we found that water—and humans—could also be a curse. One of the Land-Rover's four-gallon jerrycans had been filled at a garage in Voi with water by an unscrupulous attendant. "And dirty water at that," exclaimed my companion in his rage. The tank and carburettor had to be drained and David gave us fresh supplies of petrol from his precious stock. To be stranded in Tsavo can be a matter of life and death. One party of visitors whose car broke down in the Park actually were preparing to commit suicide when they were found nine days later.

On the way to the Tiva we passed hundreds of "skeletons" of giant baobabs in the petrified forests, their trunks ripped bare of bark by herds of ravenous elephant. Others had provided lions with lairs by boring gaping holes through the baobabs in search of sap and water.

It was part of the grim irony of Nature in Tsavo East that, in contrast to the arid area bordering the Athi River where there was water in plenty, there was rich and abundant vegetation for many miles around the Tiva, a two-hour drive from our camp. Yet the river itself was bone dry, its bed pitted with deep holes made by thirsty elephant digging three or four feet into it with their trunks for trickles of water. We sat beside that river bed unarmed, playing a card game known appropriately, perhaps, as "Idiots' Delight", while waiting for animals to come in from the surrounding country, which abounded with lion, rhino and buffalo. The river bed had been churned up as a result of frequent battles for water between enraged elephant and rhino.

On the journey back to the Athi River camp our African guide —these men and the white wardens throughout Africa have binocular-power eyesight—spotted yet another dead rhino lying beneath a tree a quarter of a mile away from the dusty track we were following. Its horns had already been cut off by tribesmen. Within half an hour we found another, lying exhausted and dying but still game enough to attempt a feeble attack on us, among the rocks of the Athi River itself and near the body of an elephant victim of the drought.

These were the first glimpses of the horrors of Tsavo East. There were many more to come.

★   ★   ★

I always endeavour to keep a respectful distance from buffalo. They have earned the reputation, which, according to some authorities, is not fully justified, of being among the three most dangerous types of animal in Africa, cunning, cruel and relentless.

We had returned to Voi headquarters and were chatting sombrely to balding, curly-haired Denis Kearney, an Assistant Warden, on the effects of the seemingly everlasting drought when there came a call for help.

Twenty miles off a buffalo cow was trapped in the thick, black mud of a dried-up lake in which two of the animals had died in suffocating agony the previous night. Ropes and a length of chain were tossed into a Land-Rover and we followed Denis's dust-trail in another vehicle as he careered away with a team of Africans. We found the vicious, terror-stricken animal in the last stages of exhaustion. With only her head and neck clear of the treacherous mud, she was still sinking slowly and there was not time to be lost if the cow was not to share the fate of her two companions.

The rescue called for that cool courage with which game guardians are so well endowed. Denis set out planks across the quagmire up to the stricken buffalo while I drove to a visitors' lodge to fetch a jerrycan of water and a tin bowl. By the time I got back Denis had roped the animal's head and horns, and crouching down he gave the parched and struggling beast a drink from the bowl and cooled and cleaned its mud-caked jaws with a rag soaked in the water. The beady-eyed, raw-necked vultures waited, ruffling their feathers in the hot sun.

The end of Denis's lasso was tied to a chain attached to the Land-Rover, and at a signal from him the African driver slipped into first gear and slowly took up the strain. Aided by a daring shove from Denis, the prostrate buffalo was dragged bodily past him out of the deadly mud trap on to hard ground. As Denis unslipped the noose and squeezed water from the rag over its distended nostrils, the buffalo staggered, snorting, to her feet.

Whatever the merits of a buffalo's reputation, gratitude does not seem to be part of its make-up—even when you save its life and stand it a drink. I had to dash to the Land-Rover as she charged erratically before climbing the bank of the lake to set out in search of the herd. "Let's hope it hasn't all been in vain and she isn't dragged down by hyenas," said Denis as we drove back. On the drive we passed a sick rhino covered in brick-red dust and two forlorn elephant calves weakly searching for food.

*　　*　　*

From Voi we again travelled up country in Tsavo East to meet another of David Sheldrick's assistant wardens, hawk-eyed and hairily-blonde, Peter Jenkins, who is Kenya-born and had been fourteen years in the Park, I found him seated on a log in his bivouac camp by the dry Tiva River, briefing a patrol of African game rangers about to set out on a raid against elephant and rhino poachers. On some patrols camels are used. At Jenkins's feet were the horns of a rhino killed by elephant battling for waterholes in the river bed, and the tusks of an elephant fatally injured when it pulled down a baobab tree with its trunk.

At that time, in late 1961, Peter Jenkins and the other white wardens in the Colony were tirelessly carrying on their work in a vacuum of the transition from a predominantly European to an African government.

"Some Africans in Kenya today are killing elephant out of sheer bloody-mindedness aroused by nationalist politics," said Peter. "They do not even bother to take the tusks. African politicians should realize they are sitting on a gold mine in our wealth of big game and wild life in general."

Kenya, he said, would be obliged to take full, properly financed conservation measures to save the game. The alternative was to destroy the lot. It was all or nothing.

"We have got to get it over to the tribesmen, particularly those on the verges of national parks, the vital need for game conservation. Tsavo has been a National Park for over fifteen years and yet a chief on the edge of the Park who wanted to send in his tribal cattle for grazing the other day did not have a clue what went on here or why."

The secret of putting down poaching, Peter emphasized, was to get at the middleman or the receiver. The police, with limited personnel, were busy with other tasks, and to help effectively in the elimination of poaching was a full-time job for a special C.I.D. squad.

"And we in the field badly need aircraft for anti-poaching operations—for spotting and to give greater mobility to the wardens and game rangers."

Peter told a horrific story of three years before when 1,200 elephant were slaughtered by poachers in one area of Tsavo. There was one dead elephant to every square mile.

Late that afternoon the ubiquitous Land-Rover, with Peter at the wheel, took us for a mile on a serpentine course along the sandy Tiva bed until we came in sight of a large herd of elephant digging for water. The carcass of a buffalo which had died in the river bed, lay in the middle of them covered in vulture droppings. A big bull elephant fought off a calf which tried to edge in at his waterhole, smacking it across the head with his trunk; over another hole two young tuskers fought. The elephant were so thirsty that they went on drinking with us in full view fourteen yards away. Others patiently waited their turn.

This was the closest he had ever been to them in a Land-Rover, said Peter.

The elephant's method of digging a waterhole is first to scrape away the sand with its front feet like a cat before the final shaft is made with the trunk. The sand is packed hard with circular motions of the trunk to prevent the hole caving in. Elephants blow out the sandy water through their trunks and drink only the clear, deeper water. "It takes a bull elephant several hours to get his fill of water from a dry river like this," explained Peter. "His average intake is thirty-eight gallons."

That night we dozed fitfully in the open on a rocky hill overlooking the Tiva. From dusk to dawn, as elephants and rhinos fought frantically over the waterholes in the river bed one hundred yards below, there was an incredible cacophony of grunting, squealing, snorting, trumpeting and clashing of horns, intermingled with the roar of lions and the coughing grunts of leopard. Sleep, except in snatches, was impossible, and Peter, stretched out on the rock in his sleeping-bag, kept a grip on his loaded rifle.

The tea-rose dawn came with the crescent moon still in the sky, and Peter pointed out several pairs of rhino still fighting over waterholes. Throughout the night they had been charging and counter-charging without either antagonist having had a drink. "How stupid can you get?" Peter asked.

A cloud of dust swirled up from the river bed as an elephant cow chased a rhino which was moving in on the waterhole where her calf was drinking. We scrambled cautiously down the rock to a two-foot-high stone wall on the river bank where we were able almost to reach out and touch the animals from what in effect was a ring-side seat at a fantastic jungle circus.

I had chosen Tsavo East as the most graphic area to highlight the disastrous, recurring impact of drought on wild life. Such are the savage contrasts of Africa that a few weeks after I had left Tsavo East, like the rest of East Africa, was blanketed by un-precedented torrential rains and floods which burst the banks of our Tiva and many other rivers. Drought-weakened cattle perished in large numbers in the deluge.

Temporary floods in no way menace the survival of game on the same scale as do persistent drought conditions. The large majority of animals merely get wet and miserable. The important factors are the conservation and supply of water for game. Kenya Game Department officials confirmed that in these floods at the end of 1961 the big game and buck headed unerringly for high ground and survived. Only rodents and lizards died.

John Collier who flew over Tsavo East at the time told me that parts looked like the original Noah's Ark scene, with dejected wild animals huddled close together on islands. "What we want now is a 'Gum-boots for Wild Animals Fund'," quipped a game warden in his plane.

When the flood-waters subsided and the toll of erosion could be seen from the air, Tsavo East looked as though giant forks had been scraped across the earth. There were tragic instances of buck bogging down fatally in the soggy fringes of waterholes.

Chapter 5

MOUNTAINS OF IVORY

IN the Arabian Nights seaport of Mombasa the Kenya Government's Ivory Room in a narrow back-street is guarded day and night by an armed, uniformed sentry. The game warden in charge there is Mr. Stanley Morris-Smith who invariably wears neatly-laundered white bush kit. He is forthright and lively-minded. Twice yearly he holds official auctions of ivory, rhino horn and hippo teeth. There were nine tons of ivory and three-quarters of a ton of rhino horn, worth in all some £30,000, stacked high in the Ivory Room when I arrived.

"Smuggling out ivory—nothing easier," Morris-Smith told me. "There are no Coast Guard systems or patrols or other watches on the seaward side. The coast is heavily indented with lonely creeks."

Ivory and rhino horns, he said, are brought down to the coastline, hidden in the bush, or buried under the floors of African huts by the poachers themselves or middlemen. Later they are collected by other persons, taken out to sea in dug-out canoes and loaded into dhows for Zanzibar, bound for the Orient. Rhino horn found its way by devious routes to China and Hong Kong where in powdered form it is sold as an aphrodisiac. The horns are also sent to Arabia where they are used to make half-pound handles of Arab daggers. There is an increasing demand for them there as a result of the country's wealth from oil. The local value of each handle is about £15.

Poached ivory is not cut up by skilled persons so the value of tusks can be reduced by at least thirty per cent. In a normal year Morris-Smith sells between 80,000 and 90,000 lb. of ivory and rhino horn. The Ivory Room houses elephant tusks and rhino

43

horns from animals poached, shot on control, or just "found".

Morris-Smith said: "We are now the main pipeline for the former Belgian Congo. In 1959 the total amount of ivory purchased by Mombasa merchants was 96,000 lb., which equals 3,000 elephants or 6,000 tusks. In 1960 we received 141,000 lb. of ivory from the Congo, but for the first three months of 1961 it was already as high as 106,000 lb. at an average of 20 lb per tusk.

"Big tusks still go to America for organ and piano keys, and to Britain for billiard balls. Medium tusks—between 20 and 40 lb.—traditionally go to India because Indian women at the time of their marriage must have one or more ivory bangles which are smashed when she dies or remarries. So there is a continual demand from that country. Small tusks go to Hong Kong for carvings. Hard ivory from the ex-Belgian Congo also goes to Hong Kong —and Japan—for carvings. Chop-sticks are made from the hollow nerve ends."

Morris-Smith added that the poacher gets about three shillings a pound for his ivory from African agents who then go to the factor who may be an Indian, usually Muslim, an Arab or another Asian. He in turn, takes it on to a main racketeer.

"It is a very highly organized business in East Africa. Its tentacles spread to the very ends of all the territories. I can tell you that three wealthy and influential business men, one in Mombasa, master-mind the whole thing, but we cannot get our hands on them. For these racketeers from their cruel trade can pay far more to people to keep quiet than we can pay them to talk. Mombasa is a smuggling hot-bed despite the fact that the price of ivory has dropped from 17·22 shillings per lb. to 14·28 shillings per lb. in under a year.

"One man was caught leaving Mombasa with two big tin trunks filled with rhino horns. Rhino have had it."

He picked up from the floor an arrow-head smeared with poison from the bark of the *Acocanthera* tree; boiled for long periods, the bark comes out like tar and its scientific name is *Glycosides of Acocanthera*. When fresh it is remarkably effective. An elephant is hit in the flank and the poison goes into the blood stream so quickly that the animal has usually gone down before the poacher reaches it to pluck out the arrow. Some poachers, with no lack of courage, will shoot an elephant from as little as fifteen yards away.

The hippo teeth in the Ivory Room came mainly from Uganda. They are used for carvings or return to Uganda transformed as "ivory" tourist souvenirs.

Morris-Smith, who has been in charge of the Ivory Room for more than four years, thumped his desk as he looked around.

"All this poached stuff comes in year after year. It is sickening. World opinion must be aroused to the value of wild game, and I feel, like so many others, that a lead should be given by the United Nations."

Adequate funds, he said, should be available for (a) game areas where the indigenous people participate actively in the preservation of *fauna*. They should derive financial benefit by way of grants for dispensary schools, help on the veterinary side and the like; and (b) to put the racketeers out of business by the employment of adequate staff and transport—"with unlimited funds to pay for information we could beat these evil people at their own game." The Mombasa Warden feels there should be an agreement between all territories of the free world to blacklist convicted persons such as white game poachers.

"And I think when a person takes out a licence to shoot elephant, rhino, lion, leopard, the greater kudu or, in fact, any major game he should be allowed only one licence in his lifetime— but this should not expire until he has killed the particular animal or animals concerned. He could be directed into areas where he would be doing the control work of the Game Departments. He could, I suggest, have a licence for such specified areas at only a nominal cost.

"Under an 'Uhuru' government the game, I fear, is going to be just 'meat on the hoof' unless something is done. I have been here for twenty years. I know the African. He is cruel, mercenary and

can see no further than today. People who were savages sixty
years ago can have no feeling for the preservation of game. What
it is costing the United Nations for any few days in the Congo
would save most of the animals."

He urges the recruitment for anti-poaching of European
personnel from white hunters who are no longer in full employment together with Africans who were formerly in the police.
There is obvious need for well-equipped anti-poaching patrols,
provided with aeroplanes or helicopters.

"In the preservation of game you have to be utterly ruthless
when you get hold of a person," Morris-Smith went on. "The
maximum penalty in Kenya, where the illegal trophy in question
concerns elephant, rhino or leopard, is a £1,000 fine or five years'
imprisonment. Where 'a vehicle, vessel, rifle or any equipment'
is used in the commission of the offence, it is automatically confiscated. I know of a man who had a *kongoni* (hartebeest) in the
back of his car and lost the car on the order of the magistrate. My
grouse is not against the fellow who kills the odd antelope for
himself and his family, but against highly-organized poaching,
particulary where poisoned arrows are used. African poachers
are now driving Land-Rovers to hunt game. . . . The picture is
gloomy. I cannot tell you how gloomy."

Morris-Smith is, however, in favour of the legitimate sportsman, who goes out for a weekend or a week. "If he is reasonably
decent and plays the game, he shoots half a dozen animals at the
most, gets off the road into remote country and disturbs the
poachers."

Morris-Smith said he probably would quit the country after
ndependence because he believes that, as a result of his efforts to
stamp out poaching, he is a marked man.

Out of the cathedral-like twilight of the Ivory Room we went
into the glaring sunshine, and down to the Indian Ocean shore,
some thirty miles from Mombasa where Moris-Smith's words of
the illicit ivory trade were translated into reality.

In a palm-fringed creek I spied on African smugglers, who were stripped to the waist. They were loading eight tusks of ivory into a dug-out canoe, which, at sunset, they paddled out to a dhow riding the swell at sea. It was a furtive, crudely-efficient and dangerous operation in which their frail craft would have had no chance against the breakers if a sudden storm had blown up.

The next day we drove eighty miles out of Mombasa into elephant country to trap a poacher. Morris-Smith, who had ordered the operation, was obliged to remain behind in the Ivory Room on urgent duties connected with another sale by auction. My companions were two African rangers of his staff, one of them a fierce and handsome corporal, Barisa Dabasa, aged thirty-one, whose face bore the tribal scars of the Waliangulu.

"Many game rangers have been poachers themselves and know all the tricks," said Morris-Smith before we left. "And African game rangers, I have found, become good preservationists."

Turning off the main Mombasa–Nairobi road, we drove for an hour and a half through dense bush to a rocky clearing. Two or three ragged Africans materialized in a matter of seconds and, to lure the elephant poacher to the spot, a message was sent to his village that I, in the guise of a European sportsman, needed a tracker for a day's hunting. After about twenty minutes the duped poacher appeared, wearing an up-turned bush hat, a stained brown jacket and *kikoi*, an Arab-type cloth skirt. There was a hand-shake and an effusive exchange of greeting with Corporal Dabasa. Then the man found himself handcuffed, and being confronted with an equally bizarrely-dressed, barefooted informer who sported a pink shirt. As the poacher and informer squatted on the ground, the Corporal began a lengthy interrogation which was punctuated by the stamping of his rifle-butt as he became increasingly vehement during the interminable African thrust and parry in which the poacher stoically protested his innocence. "Tembo (elephant) walked up to my house and died," he claimed.

Later, he admitted killing one elephant, but not two as stated by the informer. Under further questioning, he confessed that he had slaughtered seven of them, but said that the tusks had been stolen. Two hours had passed by the time the poacher, under pressure from the glowering guards, agreed to lead us to the spot where he had buried two tusks.

With the handcuffed poacher nimbly leading the way, we struck off into the trees, clambered over granite outcrops and swept through tunnels amid the bushes, halting only while Corporal Dabasa loaded his rifle to guard against poisoned-arrow attacks by other poachers. After a mile trek, we reached a hide-out among the bushes, marked by the dead ashes of camp fires. The poacher indicated a narrow gully filled with leaves and branches. A thorough search by the two game rangers revealed nothing. The poacher then pointed out two or three other places in the vicinity, but again there were no tusks. After further violent, but vain questioning, we returned to the Land-Rover beside which stood the poacher's uncomprehending wife and two children. The woman stared blankly as he was driven away between the two game rangers.

On the journey back we stopped to inspect and destroy a long fence of thorn trees set up by African poachers who drive zebra, kudu, *kongoni* and other wild animals through gaps in which spring-traps of bent saplings and wire nooses have been set.

We took the poacher to Morris-Smith's bungalow home near the lighthouse in Mombasa. Against the scullery wall of the house he sat with an air of apparent resignation. It took time to unravel the whole story, but eventually we got everything clear. The police, we learned, had arrested a man found in possession of ivory in the district which we had visited, but had not been able to capture the hunter.

Our man was the hunter.

Above: The ivory sale room at Dar-es-Salaam; the long rows of tusks bear witness to the slaughter of the elephant. The small size of the majority tells how few of the animals live to any great age.

Right: When the rangers came this baby elephant was starving; its mother had fallen to a poacher's arrow.

Charles "Tuffy" Marshall has been leading an unrelenting struggle against poachers for many years in Tsavo (see page 54). The large assortment of traps is but a small selection from what he and his rangers have taken from poachers. Yet the slaughter these implements make is small by comparison with the carnage caused by poisoned arrows and the poachers' commonest device, a running noose of wire.

(See facing page 160.)

Above: The ivory sale room at Dar-es-Salaam; the long rows of tusks bear witness to the slaughter of the elephant. The small size of the majority tells how few of the animals live to any great age.

Right: When the rangers came this baby elephant was starving; its mother had fallen to a poacher's arrow.

Charles "Tuffy" Marshall has been leading an unrelenting struggle against poachers for many years in Tsavo (see page 54). The large assortment of traps is but a small selection from what he and his rangers have taken from poachers. Yet the slaughter these implements make is small by comparison with the carnage caused by poisoned arrows and the poachers' commonest device, a running noose of wire.

(See facing page 160.)

Chapter 6

KENYATTA AND THE PRINCE

THE over-worked and under-paid game wardens of Kenya were worried and distressed because no African political leader had spoken out in favour of saving the country's wealth of wild game. Men like Mr. Tom Mboya were said to have expressed private views on the necessity of extending financial aid and scientific measures to ensure game preservation after an African government came into power, but balked at expressing their sentiments in the Legislative Assembly, fearing that it would be tantamount to committing political suicide.

Since his release from rustication a few weeks before, the elderly and flamboyant African leader Jomo ("Burning Spear") Kenyatta had delivered many orations—but none touched on the question of the fate of the animals when "Uhuru" would be a fact.

I left Nairobi and drove thirty miles to the gaggle of thatched huts and Indian stores of the village of Gatandu where Mr. Kenyatta had a bungalow home on the crown of the hill among his Kikuyu people. Turning off the main road, I travelled for three quarters of a mile along a steep mud-track until, within sight of the bungalow, I was stopped by an African guard manning a road barrier of the pole and concrete-weight type used at many Customs and Immigration posts in Africa. At the mention of Mr. Kenyatta's name, and after a hasty glance at my Press credentials, the guard raised the pole and I was allowed to drive to a gate in the tall wire fence which surrounded the neat, green-and-white painted house.

The wearing of uniforms by supporters of African political parties in Kenya had at that time been banned. A group of Mr. Kenyatta's personal "police" ranged on either side of the gate were, however, uniformly dressed in light-brown dungarees.

D

There was no sign of Mr. Kenyatta. A smartly-dressed, well-spoken African secretary hurried out, scattering a pair of goats which were cropping the sparse grass. He was polite, non-committal and suspicious until I stressed that my visit was not connected with the run-of-the-mill of African politics, and pointed out that whatever Mr. Kenyatta might have to say on the question of game conservation would be of vital importance to Kenya and could profoundly influence other African nations.

The secretary went back into the house, and after a wait of ten minutes I was ushered into Mr. Kenyatta's study, on the wall of which was the shield-mounted head of a kudu. By then a crowd of forty or fifty African men and women —disciples of "Burning Spear"—had gathered outside the bungalow and, punctuated by cries of "Kenyatta" and the throbbing of drums, sang shrill chants in praise of their leader.

He strode into the study wearing a gorgeously-beaded fez-style cap and waving an intricately carved fly-switch, of the type made from wildebeest tails and carried by chiefs. His handshake was surprisingly strong and firm for an old man. And this, with his steely, appraising stare, reflected the power of his personality.

Mr. Kenyatta slumped into a chair, waved me to a seat opposite and after staring round the study, said swiftly and without prompting: "It is very important that we should preserve our game. . . . It is a great asset, economically and otherwise, and we must protect and ensure the survival of the animals we have . . . they are part and parcel of the prosperity of our country and in fact of Africa in general."

With a dig at big-game hunting by white men, he added: "We do not want the animals to be shot." He waved a hand towards a mounted elephant foot set on a sideboard, and at a zebra foot cigarette lighter and a buck foot bedside lamp standard—gifts from admirers—on a table in another part of the study.

"I like wild animals very much," he said as the secretary nodded agreement. "They are part of our heritage. I often go to the Nairobi park to see them."

This declaration Mr. Kenyatta obviously felt set the seal on his concern and regard for the wild creatures of his homeland. For another handshake and a swish of the fly switch signified dismissal, and Mr. Kenyatta returned to his desk in an adjoining room to continue the last stages in a bitter campaign for independence of which he was then the figurehead. Outside the cries of "Kenyatta, Kenyatta" went on in the sunlight. . . . Six months later members of Kenyatta's Kenya African National Union called in the Kenya Legislative Council in Nairobi for the death sentence to be imposed on receivers of wild life trophies. They were supported by Mr. J. Keen, M.L.C., who said there should be capital punishment for receivers and long-term prison sentences for poachers who killed game, particularly rhino.

*   *   *

Two hours later, after returning to Nairobi and driving out through the city to the exclusive white suburb of Langata, I was being welcomed at his elegant home by one of the world's greatest hunters who had been dubbed by some of his wealthy neighbours as "The Killer".

The fierce-sounding title had conjured up the vision of a steely, ruthless individual, burning with blood lust. My host, however, the 6 ft. 5 in. tall Prince Franz Josef Windish-Graetz, great grandson of the Emperor Franz Josef, entertained me that afternoon with a sparkling charm and courtliness—the hallmarks of the aristocrat and gentleman of a graceful, bygone day—so rarely encountered in this brash and feverish decade.

Every room in his house is crammed, like a museum, with big and small game trophies which are but a minor portion of his overall collection. The Prince at one time held six world records in respect of his hunting trophies—he is acknowledged by white hunters and game wardens throughout East Africa to be "a superb shot"—and his record for a fine specimen of a European brown bear in the Carpathian Mountains in 1939 is still unbeaten. The mounted head and skin of the bear hangs on a wall of his lounge together with heads of Roan antelope, gazelles, reedbuck and East African eland. An arch at one end of the lounge was framed with the 9ft. 6 in. and 9 ft. 4 in. tusks of an elephant which he had shot on the Athi River, 200 miles from Nairobi, in 1955. Another room contains the mounted skins of tigers bagged in India.

The Prince is unique among white hunters in that he does not wear the bracelet of black, wiry hair from the tail of an elephant. In the early days in Africa the witchdoctors advised their people that if these hairs from an elephant's tail could be snatched from the beast before it died—after being speared or shot with arrows—it would not be able to return from the spirit world to wreak vengeance on its attackers. Today, such bracelets are commonly worn as good luck charms both by white hunters who have had to face, through the gun sights, many an enraged elephant, and by tourists whose encounters have probably been restricted to zoos or in the safety of a *safari* vehicle at a distance of some hundreds of yards.

Above the head of the Prince's bed there hangs from a golden chain a 101½ lb. tusk of one of his elephant victims. "They say that this is my sword of Damocles and that one day the tusk will fall and kill me in revenge for the fact that in my time I have shot everything," he remarked with a wry smile. It is also generally believed in Kenya that the Prince's passion for hunting is psychological, the one way in which, deprived of castles and legions of servants, he can recapture the grandeur of his royal ancestry. He came to the Colony in 1947 and was planning to leave before "Uhuru". "The Africans killed one million head of game in Tanganyika last year," he said. "The Africans hate us, you know. The white man in Africa and all over the world is doomed. East Africa is finished and I must leave here soon. There will be world communism in a quarter of a century."

The Prince has kept written records of the tens of thousands of animals he has shot in his hunting career. Today his title of "The Killer" is hardly justified for he now shoots only wild birds, and acknowledges every beast as "a monument of Nature".

Chapter 7

"GARDEN WITHOUT FLOWERS"

During my stay in Kenya I was privileged to meet four men with widely divergent personalities and individual backgrounds who yet shared a deep love and concern for Africa's wild life.

CROUCHED in a low fork of a fever tree, the leopard tore savagely at a dead reedbuck. Three feet below, poised on the tree trunk, my photographer companion snapped pictures in colour as I directed a flash-light into the leopard's yellow-green eyes. Its meal finished, the leopard slithered down the tree between the photographer's legs to tussle on the grass with a year-old male lion which had been nuzzling my trouser leg.

We were in East African bush country, but the animals which were our photographic subjects on this occasion were the half-tame pets of Italian-born Francesco Bisleti, aged 34, who owns a 54,000-acre ranch near the flamingo lake at Naivasha. On his ranch he keeps 6,000 head of cattle and 14,000 sheep.

When I called on Mr. Bisleti a leopard and cheetah were playing hide-and-seek among the rose bushes on the lawn at the front of his house. Although a game hunter himself, volatile Mr. Bisleti, who has a large lounge containing skins, heads and other trophies, keeps an open zoo on his estate in which he protects wild animals saved from the bush until they are old, or strong enough to be set free in game parks and animal reserves. He had four other leopards, said to be the hardest animals to tame, in large cages on the ranch.

The female leopard, Tina, which we photographed in the tree near the house, had been reared by Mr. Bisleti from a cub. "I have no trouble with burglars," he said.

His fully-grown pet cheetah, Tana, also runs free and hunts on his land, returning to the house each evening purring loudly.

Another leopard which Mr. Bisleti loaned to a visiting Hollywood film company is now in the San Diego Zoo.

To complete a picture terrifying to all visitors, the lion, Shaibu, is also allowed to roam loose in the grounds under the eye of Mr. Bisleti's young African animal attendant, Wambugu. The animals nip Wambugu's bare feet and pounce harmlessly on him in play. And Tina allows him to drag her by the tail.

Mr. Bisleti's dog pets, which frolic with the lion, the leopard and the cheetah, include a three-legged Alsatian and a half-breed Masai hunting dog.

"I have sometimes taken Tina with me on hunting trips," says Mr. Bisleti who came to Africa from Rome thirteen years ago. "I never shoot on the farm itself where I have also given protection to buffalo, zebra, steenbok, duikers and gazelles."

★   ★   ★

From Naivasha I travelled to Tsavo West Royal National Park. The kindly, philosophical king of this 4,000-square-mile protected territory is a pipe-puffing giant, Warden Charles "Tuffy" Marshall. To him elephant families browsing in the garden of his villa in the Park is a common sight.

"Tuffy" showed me a poster appealing for Kenya's "Water for Wild Animals Fund" which read piquantly: "Why not adopt an elephant? Three thousand elephants in Tsavo need a drink. For 36s. or $5 you can keep an elephant in drinks for a year (baby elephants half price)." The poster was illustrated with a poignant photograph of an elephant and her calf digging for water in the bed of a dried-up river.

Using money from the fund, much of which has come from Britain and America, "Tuffy" had put down boreholes in Tsavo West from which ran pipelines to feed artificial waterholes—some merely pools with low cement walls—for the elephant and other big and small game. Each borehole cost an average of £1,500 and each pool provides drinking water for some forty to fifty elephant a day.

He was the pioneer of a short-lived scheme to break the current drought by "seeding" clouds with meteorological balloons carrying dry ice released from the tallest hill in Tsavo West. The Government clamped down swiftly when it discovered that "Tuffy's" balloons would float in the path of airliners flying between Nairobi and Mombasa.

*   *   *

Everywhere the wild life was being threatened, but near Eldoret I found a verdant haven among the rolling Kenya highlands.

In 1953, when giraffe in the area were ravaging the agricultural crops, the Kenya Game Department condemned the animals to death by shooting at the insistence of angry white farmers. Hearing of this, 73-year-old Mr. Alexander Douglas, millionaire widower and owner of an 18,000-acre cattle ranch, bought seventy-two giraffe—"at much less than the £15 a head the Game Department tried to squeeze out of me," he chuckled. He allowed them to roam on his land. Today Mr. Douglas has a total of more than 120 giraffe of all ages on the ranch. He also owns 5,000 head of cattle which mingle with them and with waterbuck, reedbuck, hartebeest and oribi, which is a miniature antelope.

Mr. Douglas, born in the Cape Colony, was trained as a lawyer, but came to Kenya as a white hunter. In his heyday he speared lions in Mozambique in African fashion. Today on his big estate he lives not in a mansion but in a humble wooden shack.

"They were all man-eaters, and as the hunter I often became the hunted," said this gruff, but kindly, saviour of the game. "I had my fill of killing."

Mr. Douglas daily wears a grimy, double bush-hat, cattle-dip-stained pullover and khaki trousers held up by a beaded Masai belt and is known, often jealously, sometimes affectionately, by his farmer neighbours as "Dirty Douglas". He has been unpopular with whites and Africans alike for keeping the giraffe families.

"Something practical—even in my small way—has to be done

in the fight to save the game," he remarked. "I feel very strongly that America, with all her financial resources, must give a greater lead to the world, and without any strings at that, in saving our wild life from disaster. Why, the plateau here was black with game only ten years ago, and now most of the wild animals in the area are only to be found on my ranch."

It is a strange, but moving, sight to see his meadows filled with giraffe while cattle browse nearby. "These graceful creatures and their beauty keep me from being lonely," said the old man who speaks fifteen African languages and whose mother was a descendant of George ("Rocket") Stephenson.

At sunrise, under a crimson canopy of clouds, we watched a courtship dance in the middle of one herd of a young male and female giraffe, weaving, butting, circling and sweeping the ground with their heads while others rose up on their haunches and made away with their characteristic and stately undulating motion to feed off the trees.

According to Dr. L. S. B. Leakey, curator of the Coryndon Museum in Nairobi, it is a common fallacy that a giraffe never lies down. "He does so frequently, even at times stretching his neck along the ground to rest it," states Dr. Leakey.

Giraffe herds, led by handsome bulls, have become virtually tame on Mr. Douglas's ranch and can be approached to within a few yards before they amble off, with the grace of Ziegfeld Follies girls, without any sign of panic. We put down two 10 lb. blocks of rock salt and sprinkled the grass with coarse salt to concentrate the animals in one spot for photographs, and later Mr. Douglas, John Collier and I rounded up more than fifty giraffe on foot and drove them to high ground for other pictures.

*   *   *

I travelled on to Nairobi Royal National Park where lions stalk, kill and mate at no more than a ten-minute drive from the city.

The oldest inhabitants of the Park are the lions "Blondie" and

"Brunette" which, like the others, treat with complete indifference the scores of visitors constantly ringing them in cars when they are eating or resting. These visitors find it hard to believe that, with the lions' placid poses and a comfortingly clear view of the city in the background, the big cats are inherently dangerous. African game rangers patrol the Park on bicycles every day in order to obtain the fullest possible information regarding the habits and movements of the game population. It is recorded that "Blondie" once ambushed a cycle-riding ranger. She snatched his haversack containing bottles of milk: these she smashed; the haversack was torn to shreds. Not long after this "Blondie" chased another ranger. Though the man was on foot he was able to escape into the forest—but the lioness got his hat.

On another occasion two big lions in the Park known as "The Spivs" attacked a ranger who abandoned his bicycle and his hat to hide in a hut. An official report on the incident states: "A number of attempts to recover his property failed and visitors to the Park that afternoon were horrified to see a bicycle and a hat lying beside two lions, with no trace of the owner."

A family of lions has chased cars, travelling at sixty miles an hour, along the main Nairobi-Mombasa road which runs parallel with the boundary of the Park.

I was watching a female baboon cradling a baby in her arms like a human child when a large *safari* car with a rhino horn mounted on the bonnet drove up and the baboon made off with the youngster clinging upside down to her belly.

Giraffe, impala and zebra formed an appropriate background as Colonel Mervyn H. Cowie, Director of the Royal National Parks of Kenya, stepped out of the car to greet me. We toured the Park together and I viewed with increasing dismay the number of whitened skeletons here and there of wild animals which had died in the drought. And at that time too, the game breeding rate showed a marked decline in Kenya because of the rate at which land was being brought under cultivation. There was also markedly-increased poaching and Colonel Cowie was doubtful whether conditions would allow the numbers of the game to recover from anticipated "frightful losses".

Charming, forthright and of distinguished appearance, Colonel Cowie has a well-deserved reputation as one of the leading game experts of our time. On the subject of the dangers of extinction of Africa's wild life, he rarely minces words whether governments or individuals are concerned. I asked Colonel Cowie to sum up the game situation.

"Fifty years ago most of East Africa carried large populations of wild animals," he said. "I have personally seen them roaming in their thousands over land which is now under crops or used for livestock. The places in which wild animals can continue to live are now restricted to the few national parks and other places where the march of development has not reached."

The density of wild animals in the areas which still remained available to them was not any greater per square mile than it apparently was fifty years ago. The obvious conclusion was that the number of wild animals in East Africa had declined in direct proportion to the amount of land which has been taken over for man's requirements.

"As a rough estimate this can be taken as being 90 per cent," Colonel Cowie went on. "The rules of Nature which govern the equilibrium between predators and their prey, between herbivores and vegetation, and between man and wild animals, no longer apply. Thus, the areas in which wild animals still survive must be managed by man using all the scientific information and experience that can be made available. In other words, the day has gone when wild animals can be protected in vast areas simply by putting a line on a map and saying by decree 'No Shooting'.

"In my opinion, lawful hunting does not do much damage to the stock of game populations. It is strictly controlled and usually in the hands of experienced professional hunters whose living depends on the survival of the animals. Unlawful hunting, in other words poaching, is on the contrary, the greatest physical threat to the survival of all creatures in East Africa.

"When man lived as a primitive predator, his hunting was mainly for food or for wild animal products, for his personal use. In the last twenty years, and more so within the last ten years, poaching has changed its character and become a huge racket, designed to produce money for the poacher which he usually converts into liquor, greater profits for the middle-man or promoter, and vast profits for the Asian trader who illicitly exports the trophies. It is not true to say that the white man in his period of administration of East Africa has judged the traditional pursuits of wild men suddenly to be an unlawful activity. The object of such hunting has entirely changed. It is not done now of necessity or for food, but merely for the conversion of part of Nature's bounty into a sordid profiteering business involving the most indescribable cruelty and wanton destruction. Hunting without licence is therefore made unlawful because it threatens the very existence of the stocks from which we must draw for future generations.

"Civilized people grow flowers and lawns in front of their houses, whereas Africans prefer to plant crops or have cattle and goats. It is unlikely that the African will recognize any aesthetic, cultural or educational value in the preservation of wild life, until he reaches the stage of civilized development, when he too will like to see flowers in his garden."

There was, however, a tangible value of wild life in the extent to which it was the main attraction to tempt people to cross the world and spend their money as tourists in East Africa. This was the reason, even if there was no other reason, for saying to the African politicians that they must preserve those remnants of wild life if they wished to safeguard and reinforce one of the main pillars in the economy. The money spent by tourists visiting East Africa in the course of a year had been assessed by the East African Travel Association as being at least £7,000,000. This was capable of considerable expansion if African governments set out to get the trade. The money spent went into the pockets of a great variety of people, including a share which went to the government in the form of licences and indirect taxations.

Colonel Cowie added: "I foresee that the only way to preserve a reasonable variety and quantity of wild animals in East Africa will be to direct effective protective measures to defined areas which will have to be carefully managed and may eventually have to be fenced. Outside of such areas there is little prospect of preserving wild life at all, and probably rightly so if one recognizes that wild life is a natural resource which must be related to the correct use of land.

"I am not convinced that game farming has any great prospect in East Africa because, although in theory it has infinite merit, in practice I see many difficulties. On the one hand it is perfectly logical to convert surplus animal meat into useful protein for starving millions, particularly when it can be drawn from areas which have little hope of supporting either crops or livestock. On the other hand, there are many traditional, religious and tribal prejudices against eating certain kinds of wild animal. Moreover, there are such insuperable problems in transporting the products, either in a dried or canned form, to their markets that I cannot see such a scheme working on a big scale without infinitely more market research and a great change of outlook in many of the dense centres of African population.

"As to the future, I believe there is a hope that the emerging African governments in this part of Africa may see the sense of safeguarding one of their main sources of national income, with the consequential prospect of money being made available from other countries and international sources for scientific research. Without its wild life, East Africa would have to be downgraded to an inferior tourist market; it would be like a river without water, or a garden without flowers."

*　　*　　*

At Rumuruti, close by Mount Kenya, a European farmer, Mr. F. G. Seed, who is also an honorary game warden and a prominent member of the Kenya Wild Life Society, had set aside part of the estate for the use of wild animals. This provided a practical example to his neighbours that it is possible to farm and still keep some game.

Five miles from Mr. Seed's house there is a small spring, surrounded by fever trees, which has been led into a one-acre dam and game of many varieties abound in the area.

I had a very cordial invitation to go to Rumuruti, but unfortunately, I was unable to visit Mr. Seed who subsequently provided me with extracts from a record book kept in a lodge, suitably camouflaged and roofed, set fifteen feet above the ground in a large fever tree in the game section of the farm. During the two-and-a-half years he had been operating the sanctuary, he and his guests had seen the following animals of interest; lion seventy-two times; rhino eight times; buffalo "too often to be counted"; elephant ten times, and on one occasion a herd of fifty-six and a herd of twenty-four both in one night; waterbuck at every visit; impala, Kenya hartebeest, eland, zebra, honey badgers, wild dogs, warthog, giraffe, baboons, vervet monkeys, the rare aardwolf, an occasional jackal and a white-tailed mongoose.

Mr. Seed, as a result of his observations from the tree-lodge, claims that a pride of lion on the hunt, making low grunts to one another, sometimes like a suppressed moan, have uncanny powers as ventriloquists to outwit their prey.

Chapter 8

BEHIND BARS

WITHIN ten years there may not be a single rhino left in Kenya —that is in an area which is as big as France and Belgium combined. And all because of a myth. Rhino horn is not horn, but thick, matted hair fibre and hide. Powdered and taken like snuff, it has the false reputation among wealthy old men of Far Eastern countries of being powerful sexual stimulant and elixer of youth. This illusion, created by the phallic symbolism of the rhino horn,

has persisted for decades and is bringing these giant African survivors of the Prehistoric Ages to the brink of extinction.

Each horn ranges in weight, according to age and type, from
3 to 12 lb., and on a shrinking market the price paid to poachers
or Asian and Somali middlemen in Mombasa before the horns
start their voyage across the Indian Ocean is now as high as £6 or
£7 a pound, a rich reward for the risks of rhino killing taken by
the tribesmen to whom as little as £50 is considerable wealth.

Some professional hunters say that the rhino, being myopic and
a sound sleeper, is the easiest of the big-game animals to kill.

"If he doesn't get wind of the hunter, the chances are he knows
nothing at all until it is too late," said the well-known Nairobi
hunter, Sydney Downey.

In 1960 the carcasses of 135 poached rhino were found by
Kenya game wardens, although it is believed the number lost to
spears and poison arrows was in the region of 300. The poacher
makes a daring rush and thrusts his spear through the animal's
shoulder into its heart, taking only the horns and spurning the
meat. During 1961 poaching was officially described as "very
much worse every week and increasing all the time". Major Ian
Grimwood said then: "In some areas rhino won't last another
year. In others rhino may hold out for a while, but I will be very
surprised if there is a rhino alive in Kenya in ten years time."

On the Kitui-Machakos border thirty rhino carcasses and
skeletons had been found in June and July of that year. One
pitiful survivor, in pain from a deep spear-wound which failed to
kill, attacked and gored an African woman. In Kamba, Meru,
Embu and Theraka country the rhino had "almost gone". Outside the parks, game wardens reported up to ten dead rhino each
month. Because of a financial crisis, Game Department funds had
been cut, leaving some stations without wardens and providing
poachers with free fields of operation.

The Game Department could not afford to pay informers for
information to smash the trading syndicates and put the poaching
gangs out of business. One man visited the Department and

offered to provide evidence to convict an Asian ivory horn trader. It could not afford the sum he named, and he went away—only to return several days later to boast that he had been given double the amount he had asked by a traders' ring to keep silent.

Because of their plight and swiftly dwindling numbers, rhino are the principal targets in various types of trapping and rescue operations in East and Central Africa.

Professional trappers who capture the temperamental and aggressive beasts for zoos in America and Europe, using nets of thick rope or lassoing them from lorries, justify their operations with the pessimistic claim that the day is not far off when many of Africa's animal species will be able to be seen only behind bars.

Since Rhodesia's "Operation Noah" on Lake Kariba showed the way, considerable progress has been made with drugs which can be used to render animals unconscious long enough to truss them up or crate them. Early experiments with drugs like nicotine and curare produced a certain measure of success, it is stated, but the margin between the toxic and the anaesthetic effects was usually too narrow. The result was that an overdose would kill while a weak injection would merely make a rhino more truculent towards its would-be captor.

Kenya Game Department wardens successfully tested a new drug, sernyl, in the field. An entire herd of Uganda kob was transferred to a new area by this means, while in the gameland between Nairobi and Mombasa rhino have been drugged and captured. The weapon used is a modern version of the old-time crossbow developed by a Nairobi architect appropriately named Chris Archer and used by men like ginger-bearded Warden Nick Carter to fire drug-laden syringes with accuracy into the weak spots in the animal's armour just below the shoulder.

An effective range of up to 100 yards can be reached by this powerful, precision crossbow, firing a "dart" which consists of a plunger and needle combining to make a sturdy syringe-missile. Animals can be rendered unconscious for several hours or even longer, depending on the dosage.

Sernyl generally anaesthetizes the animal long enough for it to be trussed up and crated before it wakes up, and then there are several more hours before full consciousness is regained.

Nick, swinging his crossbow and looking like the modern version of a medieval soldier of fortune, showed me round his five tree-trunk stockades in the game country 100 miles from Nairobi. There was a crate, each bearing a painted nameplate, at the entrance to every stockade or *boma* which housed a male or female rhino trapped by a shot from Nick's crossbow. One animal, because of her comparatively shapely lines, was named "Diana" after Diana Dors. Another had escaped the day before and been recaptured five miles away.

"These are all being shipped from Mombasa to the Republic of South Africa where they will re-stock Addo Park in the Cape," said Nick who talks to his charges like children. "They are getting more and more difficult to preserve in this part of the world and I am only too glad to find a safe new home for them."

In many parts of Africa it has become necessary to move animals, like those for Addo, to new areas where they will be afforded protection or to new grazing grounds where there is still freedom of movement and room for the breeding herds.

The ground-grazing, square-lipped white rhino, which are grey and not white, are in any numbers now confined to parts of South Africa and the Sudan, but a colony of about twenty was found in northern Uganda's Madi District of the West Nile, hard by the Congo and Sudan borders, and it was decided to transfer these survivors from poachers' raids to the Murchison Falls National Park some 200 miles away.

There are brave, swashbuckling men in East Africa who cherish wild animals and make a precarious living, physically if not financially, out of handling such perilous and merciful jobs. Their stock-in-trade is a souped-up truck or lorry, a noose on the end of a wooden pole, coils of stout rope and an iron nerve. The Nairobi team which transferred the Madi white rhino to Murchison were typical, using a catching truck which had been charged so often

Alexander Douglas (*left*) owns an 18,000-acre cattle ranch in Kenya. In 1953, when giraffe were ravaging agricultural crops, he bought 72 of the animals to save them from shooting. Today there are more than 120 giraffe on his land: but whereas ten years ago the area abounded in game of many kinds, now almost the only wild animals there are those to which "Dirty Douglas" gives protection.

See page 55.

Right: Colonel Mervyn H. Cowie Director of the Royal National Parks of Kenya, feeding oranges to two orphan baby elephants. An account of his views will be found on pages 57–60.

Above: Paul "Zimmy" Zimmerman is a taxidermist. He came to Kenya in 1929 and now has some 130 trained African assistants in his workshops near Nairobi. See Chapter 9.

Below: Some of Paul Zimmerman's skilled African assistants at work.

by rhino travelling at anything up to twenty miles an hour that the bodywork, bonnet, mudguards and tyres were so full of holes made with their horns that it resembled a mobile pepper-pot.

The technique in these rhino rodeos is first to "hook" the animal from the open truck by slipping the noose over its horn, drawing the rope tight by lashing it round a tree-trunk bolted to the side of the bouncing vehicle and then for one of the team of catchers to leap off and secure the fury's hind legs. After the animal has been thrown by the drag of the truck, the rhino's forefeet are fettered and the captive is drawn up along the steel rollers of a ramp into a carrying truck by a winch. It all sounds reasonably straight-forward and simple in theory, but scarred men and vehicles bear testimony that Hell hath no fury like a rhino snared.

Five thousand miles away from us a keeper in the Bristol Zoo— the first man in Britain to do so—was nervously milking "Stephanie", a two-ton common or black rhino, in her pen while her young calf looked on. This was part of an experiment to try to save East Africa's stricken rhino population. "Stephanie's" milk was analysed in a bid to find a substitute which could be used to feed baby rhinos whose mothers have died.

Chapter 9

MUTE MENAGERIE

A LARGE plot on the outskirts of Nairobi was the end of the trail for tens of thousands of wild animals—the single-storey brick-and-wood workshops of Paul ("Zimmy") Zimmerman, a gnome-like figure with spectacles pushed back on to the crown of his balding head. Into the skilled hands of 65-year-old "Zimmy" come most of the hunters' trophies shot in East, Central and West Africa by Eastern maharajahs, international statesmen, British millionaires, American film stars, dukes and diplomats. "Zimmy" is a taxidermist who proudly regards himself as a "sculptor" preserving the creatures' dignity in death.

"I am bitterly opposed to any *indiscriminate* killing of game," said the old man, with obvious sincerity. "No hunter should ever forget that all animals, like himself, have a right to live, and that all creatures are given in trust to us by God. So when a man has the urge to kill he should at least make sure he knows the simple methods on how best to preserve a trophy."

The skinning of the animal, according to him, must be done immediately after the kill; the skin itself should be salted and folded inward without delay. Ten to 15 lb. of salt may be needed for a lion or zebra skin.

"Correctly preserved trophies result in good mounts," he says. "And surely nothing but the best workmanship should satisfy the hunter and so ease his conscience for having taken a life?"

Paul Zimmerman provides workmanship with a degree of artistry perhaps unrivalled elsewhere in the world. From boyhood he has been dedicated to the task of capturing in the true reflection of Nature the beauty of wild life. At the age of fifteen he defied his father who had planned a more sedentary career for him and went to the Wiesbaden History Museum to begin his training as a taxidermist. The only time he has been anything but a taxidermist was during the First World War, when he served as a soldier in the German Army.

"Zimmy" came to Kenya in 1929 to set up in business—a move which involved his going on long and arduous *safaris* for observation and collection in the jungles of the Congo, the Sudan and Equatorial Africa. He tried in vain, roaming naked among the Congo's swamps and tall elephant grass, to capture a specimen of the rare okapi.

A huge gorilla which was shot among the Mountains of the Moon was the subject of one of his greatest feats of taxidermy. The skin of the beast was—like all the others he prepares—placed around a *papier-mâché* cast, known as the *mannikin*, based on a clay model that, using his years of experience and knowledge of bone structures, dimensions and shapes of wild animals, he had sculptured to exact measurements. The finished work was terrifyingly life-like, with the gorilla in a menacing crouch.

The veteran craftsman, eagerly explaining his work in guttural tones, took me on a tour of his premises where he has 130 African assistants and some twenty Kikuyu families who sought his protection during the Mau Mau days.

"All my senior men are 100 per cent efficient," he said, "so don't let anyone tell you the black man can't be taught a delicate art."

In one crowded room we brushed by an African hammering large pins into the head of a buffalo.

"That's to preserve the natural wrinkles of the hide," explained "Zimmy". In another corner he leaned for a moment on a pile of stuffed leopards' heads and surveyed the trophies of elephant, gazelle, badger, monkey and wildebeest cluttering the walls, benches and floor. On the far side a male lion appeared to be preparing to spring.

"I sometimes think," said "Zimmy", his blue-green eyes twinkling, "what a scene it would be—a fantastic menagerie—if all the animals I have re-created were able by some magic to come running back to me."

They would return from palaces, museums, and stately homes all over the globe.

"Ach so, what a pity that cannot be," he added wistfully.

He has prepared trophies for the Smithsonian Institute, the Philadelphia and Los Angeles museums, and several American and British universities.

His strangest order orginated, of course, from Hollywood. It was for *half* a rhino, the half with the horn pointed like a lance and piggy eyes glinting with menace. It was used for publicity stunts and advertising campaigns for the film *Hatari* ("Danger") which was shot in adjoining Tanganyika.

As I strolled through the workshops and grounds with "Zimmy", skirting plaster casts of hippo, buffalo and buck skulls drying in the sun and zebra and cheetah skins pegged out in the first stages of treatment, Mr. Len Young, head of the Photographic Unit of East African Railways and Harbours, arrived with the head of a large lion under his arm. This was the stuffed remains of "Bwana Devil"—the animal which had seized its victims from railway carriages and inspired America's first 3-D movie of that name. The head had been brought in from the Railway Club for a skin graft where a patch of mane had been cut out by a witless souvenir hunter.

In a low-ceilinged warehouse scores of Africans were at work softening hundreds of skins of animals by kneading them patiently, hour after hour, with their hands. Their mascot was the unmounted head of a lion which had a distinct leer and a woosy eye. "Shot when he was drunk, *bwana*," giggled one of the Africans.

On the steps a Kikuyu in a brown smock was acting as a manicurist to a mammoth—carefully painting the toes of an elephant's foot with shellac.

Packing cases of all sizes, sealed and labelled or awaiting their model occupants, were everywhere.

"Nothing is rushed here," said "Zimmy", peering round at groups of his workmen. "After all, we are creating images of wild life for generations to come. Although, with so much trouble in the world and a game trophy becoming more and more of a luxury, business is not what it used to be. I often tell a customer, 'I don't work for you. I work for my own satisfaction'. That's what counts, even though mine is literally a dying profession. For each trophy that is brought to me as a 'skin-modeller' has to be rebuilt and given the stance and expression of fierceness, fear or docility which befits the type and size of an animal.

"The nostrils, eye-lids, ears and toes—removing the cartilages and leaving just enough skin to manipulate—are the most difficult jobs. But it's all a slow and painstaking business, as you see."

He added: "I hate to see the brave dignity of a wild animal ruined by callous or careless treatment after it has been killed by the hunter."

In the yard were serried ranks of elephants' feet and legs which were to be cured and polished before being sold as souvenir umbrella stands, wastepaper baskets or the legs of coffee-tables, cocktail bar supports or stools.

Soles of elephant feet were destined to become tea-trays and those of rhino feet door-stops. There were also ashtray holders, cigar-boxes, candlesticks and book-ends of elephant, buffalo and eland feet.

I thought of the nightclub bar "papered" with zebra skins, of the leopard-claw ear-rings in the curio shops of Nairobi (how many creatures die as bait to lure a leopard to its doom?), and all the vulgar bric-a-brac of the tourist trade.

An elephant's right ear, "Zimmy" told me as I left, is more coveted on the souvenir market than the other because, pinned on a wall at home, it looks like the map of Africa and people can trace their travels on it for their friends.

It was a sad farewell.

SECTION TWO

*

Ethiopia

So far as game preservation is concerned, a
land of lost opportunity.

Chapter 10

MONKEY RUGS

THE Colobus monkey, handsome, shy and haughty, looks like a Lilliputian wizened man in a white cloak with his face covered with shaving lather. It lives in the high forests of Ethiopia where its black and white fur forms an effective camouflage among the pale lichen on the branches of the trees.

Colobus is a Greek word for "mutilated" which refers to the fact that this vegetarian monkey has only a small lump where the thumb should be. "Mutilated" would be a mild word to apply to the present-day state of the Colobus monkey tribes in Ethiopia. They are being freely and ruthlessly trapped and killed in great numbers for their skins, which are used to make rugs and other tourist knick-knacks.

Since the mid-nineteenth century the Colobus has been hunted in increasing degrees for its fur, and its extinction, at least in its native Ethiopia, seems but a matter of time—measured, perhaps, in only a few years. In the last six months of 1961, more than 26,000 *known* Colobus monkey skins entered Kenya on camels from Ethiopia at Moyale on the Colony's northern border. In Kenya the Colobus monkey is protected as Royal Game.

As cloaks their skins make a popular item of nationalist finery among Nairobi's black politicians. Tourists can buy the skins on the streets of the city. Between thirty and forty skins are employed in the making of a medium-sized rug which, if you know where to go in Addis Ababa's sprawling New Market that is claimed to be the biggest of its kind in Africa, can be bought for as little as £2. Leopard skins—200 came into Kenya at Moyale over the same period as the 26,000 monkey hides—are also sold there by the score at bargain prices.

The lion (a live one greets callers at the Emperor's Palace) is the

Royal emblem of Ethiopia yet game control there is notoriously lax. Over the last two or three years the Kenya authorities alone have made representations to the Ethiopians, even up to diplomatic level, to get them to institute some adequate form of control. Promises are made but little or nothing happens.

Officials in neighbouring countries say they are appalled at the continued slaughter which is causing many species of animal to disappear. Many protective regulations exist on paper, but they are seldom enforced. In a country so loosely administered that during 1961 a yellow fever epidemic raged for months in a remote southern region, causing the deaths of several thousands of people, before the health authorities in Addis got to hear of it, slackness in administering game laws is not surprising.

Little official hunting goes on. There are no *safari* companies. The few professional hunters and visiting hunters have to equip their own expeditions to regions which are difficult to reach and, because of bandits, often dangerous for strangers.

Ethiopian bureaucracy and muddle do not encourage hunters who go through the official licence procedure. An American who lived six years in Addis Ababa and used to do a lot of hunting told me: "You apply for your licence, and it might well take you four months to get it. By that time the season is closed so you can't go anyway. The simplest thing is to try and go out hunting with some high-up Ethiopian who is well in with the Emperor. Then you can shoot what you like, and be fairly sure of getting away with it."

There appears to be no official publication on the Ethiopian Government's game policy, but propaganda in a current drive to attract tourists declares that the country "provides a wide variety of hunting and shooting" and that "big game is available in many parts and licences for hunting and shooting are readily available except in the 'closed' season when breeding is taking place".

The Ministry of Agriculture is in charge of issuing hunting licences to reach some of the more interesting parts of Ethiopia, land of ancient and modern contrasts, of rolling plains, barren deserts and great mountain ranges. The most effective means of transportation recommended is by mule. It is solemnly claimed in one official pamphlet that the animals which sportsmen will find in Ethiopia include tigers. There are, however, at least two animals native to Ethiopia that can be found nowhere else in the world, the Mountain Nyala and the Walia Ibex.

The Emperor of Africa's oldest state has his own hunting reserve on the Awash Plains, and round the Awash River, between Nazareth and Awash, a game reserve has been established.

Professor George A. Petrides, a Fulbright Research Fellow, who visited Ethiopia under the auspices of the New York Zoological Society and the Conservation Foundation, travelled throughout the country by road and air and came to the conclusion that her stocks of wild game and the areas where they thrive were being materially reduced, making it difficult to establish national parks and managed hunting areas which serve both as sources of income from tourism and "living museums". He found an official lack of knowledge of the effects of land use on the country's wild animals and that officials of national and international organizations in Ethiopia had little knowledge—a tactful summing-up—of game and habitat preservation.

Professor Petrides reported: "Interest in wild life and wilderness preservation seems evident in the European community in Ethiopia. At the time of my visit efforts were being made by a British resident to organize an Ethiopian Wild Life Society, along the lines of those in Kenya and Tanganyika. Such organizations should be given every encouragement, particularly in the enrolment of interested Ethiopian leaders.

"An important need is for an early and complete survey of the nation's potential national park, wilderness and game areas. Though opinions are certain to be expressed that other economic needs are greater, permissive destruction of Ethiopia's national attractions is not progress. The economic planner frequently fails to appreciate important national needs which are not implicitly agricultural or industrial.

"There are many generations of Ethiopians to come; they should not be denied a view of their original heritage. Millions also throughout the world would come to Ethiopia through the years to take home memories of a country with unique and beautiful scenery, interesting vegetation, friendly people and thrilling wild life.

"The more industrialized economy that is coming will be interesting but not unique to visitors. Hotels and transport will help tourists while they are in the country but it is the country itself that they come to see. Destruction of natural attractions in Ethiopia is now evident. Suitable samples of natural scenery should be preserved while there are yet a few."

He urged an intensive survey of Ethiopia to determine complete needs in wild life management policy and stressed the urgency of national park preservation. Such a survey, he stated, should be conducted by individuals not with a knowledge of wild life alone but with a knowledge of wild life management as it might be integrated with forestry, agriculture, range management, watershed development and other resource uses. The ability to interpret vegetation and soil conditions to determine their permanence or rate of change owing to over-grazing and erosion was most important in such persons. They should be acquainted with land use possibilities, but geological, historical and scenic values should not be overlooked.

"The values of a national park and, perhaps, a hunting area system in Ethiopia naturally will accrue mostly to Ethiopians," Professor Petrides added. "But their example of far-sighted administration would do much to establish a progressive pattern for the management of wild life and wilderness museums on the newer independent nations throughout Africa."

For all that, the 3,000-year-old kingdom appears to have lost its opportunity of being the leader of new, free African countries in terms of progressive game policies.

SECTION THREE

*

Uganda

In September and October, 1961, the author visited Kisoro, the Murchison Falls National Park and the Queen Elizabeth National Park.

He tells how organized culling of the game herds and marketing of the resulting meat may lead to economic viability of the game reserves as well as preservation of the animal population. He tells of the crocodile poaching problem at Murchison Falls; and how from Kisoro he crossed the border into Ruanda-Urundi and went to visit the man who loves gorillas.

Chapter 11

ROAST ELEPHANT

THE London newspaper's bold headline in February, 1962, read: "Eat Wild Game, Don't Coddle It". This stark exhortation served to direct the reader's eyes to a report of a conference in Rome when world-wide organizations which are raising funds for a "Freedom from Hunger" campaign were asked by the United Nations Food and Agricultural Organization to study a plan for the controlled cropping of wild animals to provide food for hungry Africans.

Mr. Peter R. Hill, representative of the International Union for the Conservation of Nature and Natural Resources, told the conference that his organization planned to break away from the "sticky sentimentality" about Nature and wild life. The wild animals of Africa had been treated in the past "as if they were nothing more than museum or scientific specimens" and he called for their use in a sensible way. Wild animals could provide a source of protein-rich food urgently needed in many parts of Africa. This source, at the moment, remained largely untapped or wasted through the lack of proper processing and other facilities and services. In particular, there was a lack of mobile abattoirs which were essential if wild herds were to be "managed" as a food resource.

Mr. Hill said his organization realized that great reservations full of wild animals provided a dollar-winning tourist attraction in some countries of Africa. But even if more wild animals were used for food, enough could be preserved to leave a spectacle for the tourist. The herds of elephant, zebra, wildebeest, hippopotamus, buffalo and other animals in Africa, he went on, made more efficient use of available grass, herbs, shrubs and trees than did imported domestic animals. These wild animals, each grazing on its particular kind of food, were important in maintaining the established balance of Nature between plants and animals which could be seriously upset by the haphazard introduction of domestic livestock.

One-third of Africa south of the Sahara consisted of "marginal lands" where poor use of the soil had reduced fertility and production. The balance of Nature in these lands had been upset by "feckless introduction of livestock foreign to the region and ill-adapted to heat or humidity or to the local vegetation". In one region it had been estimated that a square mile of such marginal land stocked with mixed game could supply 95,000 lb. of meat compared with a mere 16,000 lb. from scrub cattle.

Mr. Hill told the conference that game processing and marketing was already receiving attention in very many parts of Africa. Problems which deserved attention included those concerned with the capturing, processing and marketing of hippo.

He concluded: "Money injected into projects aimed at controlled and carefully supervised harvesting, processing and marketing of products from wild and domesticated animals will be soundly invested. Money is needed to provide men, machines and methods. With these essential sinews, considerably more food can be produced in suitable form for the people of Africa."

His words found full support in Uganda, which is giving a strong lead in the utilization of game as both an economic crop and a recreational attraction. It was an American zoologist studying in Uganda who first formulated the idea that the country's wild life has a long-term future only if it is made to pay its way by bringing economic benefits to the local people. Game conservation, he argued, must go hand in hand with game cropping, both as a means of converting African public opinion in favour of preserving wild life and for the good management of the game itself.

Considerable research followed the zoologist's report that game could be a renewable natural resource. Four types of management schemes were investigated and later put into operation—the

Alarmed by a slight noise from the occupants of a passing canoe this
bull elephant started to charge and so provided opportunity for a
memorable photograph: it was taken in Queen Elizabeth National
Park in Uganda.

Controlled "cropping" of game prevents over-population of a reserve. If the animals that are shot are collected (*above*) and their flesh either sold to the Africans resident in the area, or sun-dried to make biltong (*below*) the wild animals can be made to contribute quite substantially to the upkeep of the land reserved to them. Experiments also are being made in the canning of game meat but it is too soon to say whether it can be marketed successfully. Biltong produced from a single zebra may fetch as much as £8.

See Chapter 17.

cropping of hippo (in and around the Queen Elizabeth National Park as described in the following chapter), Uganda kob and elephant and the establishment of controlled hunting areas.

On the Semliki Flats to the south of Lake Albert there is a population of Uganda kob estimated at about 18,000, partly resident within the Toro Game Reserve and partly outside it. Experimental cropping operations were started in February, 1961, and confined to the selective shooting of male kob in areas immediately adjoining the Game Reserve.

Orders are obtained from local butchers for from twenty to twenty-five animals at a time, and shooting, usually twice a month, is then carried out on agreed dates by the game ranger who shoots from a Land-Rover using a rifle fitted with a telescopic sight. Carcasses are taken to a central camp where they are skinned, dressed and weighed by the Game Department staff. They are then collected by the butcher in his own transport. Carcasses are purchased by weight at 8d. per lb. dressed, and the meat is retailed by the butcher in local markets at 1s. per lb. The live weight of male kob so far taken has averaged 188 lb. and they have dressed out at approximately 116 lb. each which is a dressing-out ration of 61 per cent. Carcasses have fetched an average of £4 1s. each, while good quality, uncured hides are being sold to Nairobi buyers at 25s. each, yielding an average of £5 6s. per animal.

Apart from ammunition, the cost of running the Land-Rover used in the actual cropping and the salaries of the staff, the costs are stated to be negligible and the net profit is in the region of £4 10s per animal. Local markets are limited, but the authorities state that, provided other outlets can be developed, "there seems no reason why this experiment should not be extended to a full-scale scheme giving a sustained offtake of some 1,500 animals per year, yielding an average net income of about £6,700 per annum." Proceeds from the scheme, less management costs, are paid to the Toro Local Government.

In the Bunyoro district of Uganda, lying to the south of the

Murchison Falls National Park, investigation by Fulbright research workers and others confirmed the presence of a considerable over-population of elephant. Aerial surveys showed a concentration of over 12,000 elephants in the southern portion of the Murchison Park and adjoining areas at certain times of the year. This build-up, it is stated, has been partly owing to the protection of elephant in the Murchison area and partly to the steady pressure of agricultural and other development in surrounding areas formerly, but now no longer, available to them. The consequent concentration of elephant in this comparatively restricted area resulted in heavy damage to crops and forest plantations as well as causing marked deterioration in the wild habitat. It was therefore decided to reduce the elephant population to an appropriate level by limited cropping in that area lying outside the boundaries of the Murchison Park. It is the intention to take up to 1,000 animals per year of both sexes and all age groups over an initial period of three years. Subsequently, further surveys will be carried out and the desirability of further cropping will be reviewed.

Elephants are shot by trained Game Department staff using .404 rifles. Ivory is the property of the Central Government, but 10 per cent of the proceeds from its sale is paid to the local government. Carcasses are the property of the local government, which is authorized to dispose of them through approved local contractors. At the start of the scheme the Game Department had one African contractor who purchased carcasses from the local government at £5 each and was authorised to dispose of the meat by retail sale to local buyers. The price obtained by the local government is low in comparison with hippo but, it is pointed out, this is inevitable in view of the comparative inaccessibility of the area in which the cropping is taking place and the consequent cost to the contractor of recovering carcasses.

The scheme was not in full operation by the end of 1961 because the single contractor was able to cope with only a very small number of carcasses and local markets for the meat were limited. An official report on the scheme states: "The utilization of elephant, in particular, presents considerable practical difficulties owing to the size of the animal, the type of terrain in which they are normally found, the fact that operations are almost inevitably scattered over a wide area, and the limited demand for this type of meat. At present most of the meat from this scheme is sold fresh by the contractor direct to the local inhabitants. However, if the proposed offtake is to be fully utilized it will be necessary to process meat by drying or other means and to export it to other areas."

Certain of Uganda's game areas outside the National Parks which formerly were closed reserves or sanctuaries have recently been opened to restricted and closely-controlled hunting. The maximum safe annual offtake of trophy species is determined by periodic counts and other investigations, and hunting quotas are fixed accordingly. Sportsmen wishing to hunt in these areas are issued with special permits for which they pay appropriate *per capita* fees in respect of those animals which they wish to hunt. All animals taken count against the annual quota for the area concerned, and when the quota for a particular species has been filled no further permits are issued for that species for the remainder of the season.

Fees vary according to the trophy value of the animal concerned—for example lion and leopard £24, kudu £10, buffalo £5 and so on. Revenue from these special fees, which are over and above the cost of the game licence, is credited to the local government of the district concerned. Fees are not normally charged in the case of local residents, though they are required to obtain free permits for hunting in a controlled area and any animals they take are counted against the overall quota.

Controlled hunting schemes were introduced initially in three districts in Uganda, and in general proved both successful and popular. By bringing in appreciable revenue to local authorities they provided a valuable demonstration of the economic value of wild life and resulted in a much more co-operative attitude on the part of the African inhabitants towards conservation measures.

Uganda Game Department officials emphasize that the scientific, aesthetic, educational and other advantages of game are alone unlikely to carry sufficient weight against the growing competition from agricultural and other development. They are of the opinion that: "If African wild life is to survive, it is essential that its management and utilization must be accepted as an economic and productive form of land use."

Research and pilot schemes have crystallized into a solid project —a tourism-hunting-marketing operation. The Uganda Development Company announced recently that a new company, "The Uganda Wild Life Development Company Limited," had been incorporated as a wholly-owned subsidiary of the U.D.C. to handle the effective development and exploitation of the country's game resources. The project is two-pronged. One side is the encouragement of tourism and licensed hunting, the "live" value of the game. The other is the "dead" value, the marketing of game meat. The Board of the new company was nominated by the U.D.C. and comprised the new company's own executive personnel, selected experts on conservation and ecology and others having the specialist knowledge necessary for the range of the company's activities.

The main objects of the company include providing suitably controlled exploitation of the game resources so as to achieve the maximum economic return which will accrue principally to local interests; to study and develop game as a source of cheap food to help combat the protein deficiency of the local people, and to finance and encourage the conservation of fauna and habitat in existing game areas and to develop these activities in new areas which are suitable.

The company provides facilities for tourists, principally in the controlled hunting areas, including permanent and semi-permanent accommodation, service and catering, the provision of equipment, the organization of land and water transport, and guides and couriers to cover such activities as hunting, fishing, photography, pony trekking, foot *safaris* and insect collecting.

With these facilities at its disposal, the company offers through commercial channels, its own package tours, and these are available to existing tour operators.

The company has investigated cropping schemes along the lines suggested by various study groups, and in addition has investigated the processing of game meat as food and the establishment of industries to deal with hides, skins and trophies. It is intended to process and distribute most of the game locally so that a useful contribution towards combating the protein deficiency of the indigenous people may be made. If, however, substantially higher returns could be achieved in the case of certain meats in the export market, then it will be designed to take advantage of this. It is admitted, however, that the quantities involved are not likely to be very great.

"The main object of the exercise," says Mr. D. A. Lucas of the Uganda Development Corporation, "is to demonstrate to the African local governments and the people in whose territories the gamelands lie that these lands can be of greater benefit to them under game than they would be under cattle or cultivation. Above all, we want to show that proper management and cropping of game will yield a great deal more than indiscriminate slaughter leading to extermination."

The U.D.C. feels that hunting in Africa has become a rich man's luxury with the hunter going to the pick of the few remaining areas which abound in big game. Yet there are many other areas which still have a surplus of some species of wild life and the U.D.C. is exploiting these by developing lower-cost combined tourist and hunting *safaris* for people who are not rich enough, or dedicated enough, to launch a personal hunting expedition in Africa, but who would be thrilled to combine some hunting with their sight-seeing.

Critics of the meat marketing side of the project say it is not easy to visualize this as an economic proposition. East Africa's news magazine *The Reporter* pointed out when the U.D.C. game meat plan was announced: "It depends largely on the quantity of game which the various areas could yield under optimum management conditions. As the areas have never enjoyed anything approaching these conditions, this is largely hypothetical.

"The marketing of small quantities of animal products from widely-scattered locations would certainly be much more costly than marketing the meat and products of domestic stock which can be herded and driven to a convenient processing centre. . . . The sponsors are faced with much-diminished raw material assets. Economic returns in the first few years are bound to be very scanty while proper management methods are evolved and the half-empty gamelands are restocked."

Mr. Lucas acknowledges that in the early stages game meat may have to be sold very cheaply or even given away to African families. He adds, however: "This would help to solve the problem of how to convince them that they are deriving direct benefit from the proper management of game. It would be better still if a profitable export business could be created and the profits passed on to the local government to spend for the benefit of the whole tribe or district. It may be possible to do a little of both, of course—to provide the people actually living in and around the game areas with free meat and provide their government with spending money."

Chapter 12

MERCY MURDERS

IN THE Queen Elizabeth National Park in Uganda and adjoining areas, serious deterioration of grass cover and consequent soil erosion has resulted from the growing over-population of hippo in Lakes Edward and George which are linked by the Kazinga Channel. A careful census showed a total of 15,000 hippo in the area which was considered to be greatly in excess of its safe carrying capacity. As a result it was decided to initiate cropping.

This was started in 1958 and has been carried out as two separate operations. In those areas within the Park boundaries cropping is carried out by the Park staff. The carcasses of all hippo shot are sold on the site to contractors at an average of £10 each, the proceeds going to the Park revenue. In the areas outside the Park, cropping is carried out by contractors under the supervision of the Game Department.

The first contractor was a local African butcher who was given permission for the cropping of 360 hippo during the course of a year and in return he paid the African local Government £7 10s. per hippo taken. He butchered and then removed the meat in his own transport, disposing of it by retail sale in various African populated areas within a radius of about 100 miles. There was, and is, a ready market for hippo meat at from 6d. to 1s. per lb.

It is officially reported: "So far these schemes have gone very well and no major snags or difficulties have been encountered. The total off-take from the whole area has been about 2,000 animals, and it appears probable that the hippo population could continue to sustain an off-take in the order of 1,000 animals a year indefinitely."

The snow-capped Mountains of the Moon form a back-cloth to the Queen Elizabeth Park, which is undoubtedly one of the most picturesque in Africa. At the main entrance to the Park near Kasese tourists are warned: "Although hippo appear placid and unaggressive as they bob up and down, puffing and blowing at the water's edge, no liberties can be taken with them. Certain individuals are very bad tempered, and they can move with surprising speed on land. The bulls not infrequently have tremendous battles with each other."

We were soon to learn the truth of these words in a series of—fatal to them—encounters with these huge beasts. Uganda's Senior Game Warden, brawny sun-tanned, Kenya-born, Captain Frank Poppleton, a crack shot, was carrying out a 100 per cent extermination programme in one section of the Park.

When hippo leave the water at night to feed on grass which

also provides grazing for elephant, buffalo, Uganda kob, waterbuck and other ungulates, Captain Poppleton drives among them in his Land-Rover, christened "Fly-By-Night" and shoots down every animal he picks up in the beam of a powerful spotlight.

One expert says hippo tracks have often been recorded up to twenty, or even thirty, miles from the nearest water big enough to provide them with a home.

I was to see something of Captain Poppleton's skill as a marksman the next day. Accompanied by Dr. William M. Longhurst, an American zoologist of the University of California who, under a Fulbright research scheme pioneered and piloted the hippo cropping scheme in Uganda, we drove past the bodies of five hippo shot the previous night to a pool near the Park lodge in which three were basking in the sun. Dr. Longhurst, clutching cigar-size thunder-flashes, which can blow off a man's fingers if not thrown in time, and an African game ranger remained on one side of the pool. Captain Poppleton, shouldering a high-powered hunting rifle with telescopic sights, and I moved round and hid behind a small bush on the other side. At a signal from Poppleton, the game ranger gave a series of high-pitched cries and Dr. Longhurst flung a thunder-flash which burst with a deafening crack among the hippo trio.

"Look out," exclaimed Poppleton, bringing the rifle up to his shoulder. "Hippo can charge at thirty miles an hour."

In a flurry of muddy water, two of the hippo careered past us on the bank. Captain Poppleton fired twice in split-second succession and hillocks of quivering flesh sank to the ground. Both had been killed instantly by superbly-aimed brain shots.

Dr. Longhurst snatched his rifle from the Land-Rover and fired at the surviving hippo which was still in the centre of the pool. It thrashed the water to foam in its agonies, and a second shot was required to finish it off. Poppleton's African staff later waded into the pool up to their necks to fix a chain round the head and jaws of the hippo. The body was hauled to land by a tractor to be cut up.

After Dr. Longhurst had taken blood slides and removed the eyes for age determination, Africans employed by the meat contractors set to work, hacking the dead hippos with pangas and axes while kites dived in and snatched morsels of bloody flesh. The hippo intestines and the thick and fatty skin, when boiled, are considered special delicacies by the Africans so there was competition for possession between them and Dr. Longhurst who required specimens for research into the life cycles, diseases and the parasites of hippos.

We walked down to the shore of Lake Edward where a score of hippo, one with its ears bitten off in a scrap with a rival, were rising out of the wavelets like monster sea-horses.

"In a concentrated over-population, cow hippos will kill and chew, but not eat, their own calves," said Poppleton.

He added: "The hippo cropping has resulted in a complete recovery of grazing ground which would otherwise have become a desert."

Hippo, like buffalo, have been known to come on even after receiving several shots in the body. They are the most dangerous animals in the Park and have been responsible for a high death rate among Africans living there. Frequently they have attacked men and women who were on bicycles and had overturned canoes.

Vultures pranced around the muddy body of another newly-shot bull hippo which weighed nearly 4,000 lb., tearing at its nostrils, eyes and rectum. Within two hours of the contractor and his "boys" arriving to claim this animal, no trace of it remained except a patch of red grass. A slice of hippo steak, which had been grilled over a wood fire, proved to be tangy but tasty and tender in the manner of good beef. I was told that *hippoburgers* were proving increasingly popular in African restaurants which had added them to their menus.

Dr Igor Mann of Kenya's Veterinary Department has been conducting a serious and prolonged scientific investigation into the culinary properties of hippo meat. He spent days cooking, experimenting and tasting in an hotel kitchen in Nairobi on behalf of the Uganda Government. His verdict is that hippo meat can be "very tasty" when curried. Done in this way, he stated in his report, samples of canned hippo were found to be "rich, juicy and tender"—and to contain twice as much protein as beef. He also commends dried hippo meat, and claims that the fat is "sweet smelling and quite pleasant".

The skin on a hippo joint frizzles up like pork "crackling" when roasted.

The protein requirements of nearly 40,000 Africans are covered by the 3,000,000 lb. of hippo meat available annually from cropping in the Queen Elizabeth Park, says Dr Mann who adds: "The existence of such an abundance of cheap meat in the heart of a tsetse area in the centre of Africa must be considered an enormous asset."

Hippo shooting as a form of preservation with profit is a grisly business for wardens and privileged spectators alike, so Captain Poppleton took time out to tour the Park with me and point out the wonders of an animal population living free from the menace of guns.

We found a three-foot-high, newly-born elephant, a genuine "Dumbo", standing beneath its mother and noisily drinking her milk while the rest of the herd stood protectively around them. Poppleton said he once saw a pack of sixteen hyena tearing a calf from its mother.

The quaint kongoni, we decided looks like a Thurber moose or a child's drawing of a cow. In the Land-Rover in the midst of 300 stampeding buffalo, which we herded like a mechanical sheep dog, I lost my qualms momentarily to recall the words of a Kenya warden; "He stares at you as though he owes you money or is about to seduce your wife." At that time our view was mainly confined to dusty rear-ends and flying hooves.

Teeming herds of topi, Uganda kob and buffalo on the plains were giving a wide berth to a pair of trees. We drove to beneath the first tree to find a young lioness crouched along a stout branch, her tail swishing slowly. In the other tree a hundred yards away, in a similar posture, was a young male lion, grunting in courtship to the female. At dusk he interrupted his love-making to spring from the tree and kill a young kob which he shared with the lioness.

Three lions roared over a kill by the lake below while I had dinner that night with Captain Poppleton and his Danish-born wife at their house close to the Park lodge. Captain Poppleton, a bull-fight enthusiast like Myles Turner, with whom he served in the army, was preparing to go on four months' home leave. A 45-year-old African ex-policeman, who had been eight years in the Parks' service, would take over his duties, he said, during that period at the same salary as himself.

Captain Poppleton put down his glass and hurried out into the garden. A herd of twenty elephant had come to the dinner party and were busy mangling the flowers and creepers.

The method of speeding the departure of the unwieldy and unwelcome guests was drastic and exhilarating. As I clung to the side, Captain Poppleton drove his Land-Rover, horn blowing and spotlight weaving, straight at the elephants which, trumpeting wildly, crashed off into the bushes and trees. For ten hectic minutes, bumping and lurching, we drove around in pursuit of the herd, frequently coming within a few feet of the great, grey shapes. Several times it looked as though the bull leaders would turn and attack their "cyclops" pursuer. Fortunately, they decided to continue their retreat and at last disappeared into the night.

*   *   *

Before landing in our little plane at another animal paradise in Uganda, the Murchison Falls National Park, the pilot had to buzz the airstrip several times to scare off elephant roaming on the dusty runway. Crocodiles on the sandbanks of the Victoria Nile are the chief attraction in the Park—if these scaly monsters with their evil smile can be called an attraction.

"The greatest caution must be exercised at all times in approaching the water's edge for death in a ghastly form may lurk anywhere, unseen," stated the guide book.

The danger of such a fate did not deter the local African poachers who, according to the Warden, 27-year-old, Brighton-born Roger John Wheater, a former officer in the Uganda Police, were stepping up their activities in view of the increasing demand for crocodile belly-skin at 7s. an inch.

Roger, blond and slim, showed me one of the spears, having a detachable head attached to a wire cable and a large float, used by the crocodile poachers.

"They are taking a very heavy toll with these," he said. "We have to use light boats with powerful outboard motors to stand any chance of catching the poachers. It's an endless struggle."

Earlier there had been a strange lull in crocodile poaching. The game rangers who investigated turned in a weird report. The tribesmen, it transpired, were perturbed at the number of still births and babies born blind in their village. They consulted a witchdoctor who told them it was a curse put upon them for killing a huge mother crocodile near the Falls. The spirit of the crocodile would not be appeased, he said, until a blind child had been sacrificed at the Falls. An attempt to kidnap a child for the purpose was thwarted when the father speared one of the would-be kidnappers. In the meantime the tribesmen stopped killing croco-diles for fear of further catastrophes. Despite fear of the curse, however, the pause in the killings did not last for long.

As we clambered aboard the launch *Oribi* to make the trip to the Falls, where the Nile boils in grandeur through an "eye of a needle" gorge, another enemy of the crocodile, the monitor lizard, which sneaks the eggs from nests, was basking in the sun on the bank and looking like a stuffed reptile.

The hundreds of crocodiles we approached during the trip adopted the same deceptively frozen pose on the sandbanks and in the shade of riverside trees. Some, including a ten-foot-long giant, appeared asleep but with jaws gaping wide. Roger's theory is that this is a method of cooling themselves until evening when they slither into the water to begin their mass attacks on shoals of fish.

When the launch backed away and resumed its journey, a family of hippo on another sandbank dashed for the shore in a cloud of spray. A bad-tempered bull stood his ground and made a spirited, but ineffectual, charge at the boat.

From the roof of the *Oribi*, we were able to get cine-shots from only 10 ft. away of a big male elephant idly chewing a sapling on the bank with his forefeet in the river.

That night I was given a room in the Royal bungalow in the Park and the Lodge manager insisted on ferrying me down from his office in a Land-Rover at dusk for fear of attacks by hippo coming up from the river to feed. Hearing a commotion outside my room during the night, I got up to find a hippo cropping the grass round the Royal Standard flagpole a few feet from the bungalow. The ponderous visitor was driven off by a shower of stones.

Before leaving the Park, I called at Roger Wheater's office and was introduced to his pet, a two-year-old, 1,000 lb. white rhino orphan which welcomed us into her pen with a playful toss of her horn and nuzzled Roger's hand. She had been christened "Obangi" after the West Nile district in which she and her mother had been captured by roping from a lorry. Both were to have been transferred to the safety of the Park, but the mother died on the spot from internal injuries caused during her capture.

Chapter 13

GORILLA MAN

ON the way from Murchison Falls Park to Kisoro, where Uganda has a common border with the former Belgian Congo and Ruanda-Urundi, our single-propellor charter plane flew into the terrifying blackness of a tropical storm. The clouds were slashed with broad ribbons of lightning. After a sickening tossing, we made an emergency landing at Kasese and set out for Kisoro the next morning when there was a reasonable chance that the dense clouds draping its host of volcanic mountains would have drifted away. Although we were lucky in this respect, the landing, after dodging through valleys in the teeth of blustering winds, was not without hazard.

The crude, rarely-used, grass runway was strewn with rocks but, with customary bush-pilot's skill, our pilot leapfrogged over them before making a final, shuddering touch-down. As tribesmen swarmed around the machine in this green wilderness of primitive beauty, the pilot was emphatic that we should choose another, safer airfield from which to be picked up.

Our first news was of fierce fighting near the border between Congolese and Ruanda-Urundi tribesmen—and we were to enter the Congo next day for a *safari* in the famous Parc National Albert!

A telegram to the Kasese area addressed "Gorillas" will be delivered to one of the outstanding "characters" of East Africa, a man who combines warm hospitality with a puckish humour and intelligence as befits Mine Host. Walter Baumgartel, an elderly, German-born bachelor, is proprietor of the "Travellers' Rest", a simple hotel of comfortable thatched rondavels on the doorstep of the Congo. His African cook provides some of the best meals to be had in Africa. Walter, the only white man in Kisoro, is also an author, philosopher and humanitarian whose work and exploits as an honorary game warden have earned him a prominent place in many books and journals. As a hotel owner, he is unique in having "on his books" some thirty or forty rare mountain gorillas weighing an average of 400 lb. each. They live on the forest slopes of three nearby extinct volcanoes, Muhavura, Mgahinga and Sabinio, which the Africans call "The Cooking Pots".

When Walter fled Germany as an anti-Nazi (serving later as an aerial photographer with the South African Air Force), he had no inkling that he would spend the evening of his years as voluntary "Guardian of the Gorillas", as he is now known officially, in a wild and savage part of Africa. But he has found peace, and is content as long as the occasional visitors—and over the years they have, with the Congo turmoil, become fewer and fewer—arrive to help to keep down the hotel's overheads and to pay for the airmail stamps he puts on bulky envelopes containing reports of his research work among his shaggy, fearsome-looking charges on the mountainsides, that are addressed to well-known scientists and conservationists. Impoverished biologists, including students, rarely receive a bill for their stay at the "Travellers' Rest".

Apart from the burdens of finance, Walter Baumgartel was a worried man at the time of my visit. Tribesmen will attempt to spear gorillas on the rare occasions that the giant animals raid their patch-works of crops, but casualties from this are not heavy. A more deadly and powerful enemy in the form of a "ghostly" black leopard had already taken a toll of four or five gorillas by stalking them, leaping on them in the nests and tearing out their stomachs and jugular veins before making off swiftly with each victim.

"He has developed a taste for gorilla flesh," said Walter. "He is cunning enough to disappear over the border into Ruanda-Urundi after each slaughter, and has so far evaded all my attempts to trap and kill him. This leopard is menacing the survival of the colony I have tried so many years to preserve. I have sworn to catch him before I die."

To those like myself with only a nodding acquaintance (and well back from the bars at that) with gorillas, it seems strange that Walter loves gorillas. However, he does, deeply and sincerely. He finds in them a fundamental beauty linked with creation. He approaches their lairs unarmed and wearing only shorts, sandals and an open-neck shirt for, he says, gorillas are neither ferocious nor treacherous.

"I have often come face to face with a gorilla from as little as six feet away," he says. "Then you *must* have the nerve to stare him out, retreating slowly all the while. Any sudden movement scares them and anybody who turns and runs away is courting a sticky end. A gorilla may try to throttle a man in its rage or

95

fright, or bite off an arm or leg." He claims the popular conception that male gorillas carry off African women is entirely false. They are, he says, polygamists and some have eight or more wives. Their courting and love-making, which he has watched, is touchingly human. And Walter, who talks to the great beasts in a high-pitched "hu hu hu", once witnessed a terrifying battle between two large male gorillas in a forest clearing.

"They made a tremendous racket. I think the scrap was over food and living space and not a girl-friend. It went on until the vanquished dropped dead."

He tells, too, of his African tracker Reuben finding a young gorilla huddled like a child on top of the body of its father which shunned by the females, had wandered off to die from gastro-enteritis. The baby, which would have become a victim of the black leopard, was seized and bound by Walter and his Africans and shipped to the London Zoo.

Below: During the heat of the day lions like to lie in the shade; they move only to keep within the shadow. On the Ishasha Flats in Uganda there is now little or no ground-level protection from the sun. So lions here have to climb into the trees to find shelter. Sometimes an onlooker may locate the great cat by a sight of its tail hanging down below a branch.

The photograph *above* was taken at sundown as a pregnant lioness stalked to the ground to hunt.

Above: A family of elephants at a lake in the Parc National Albert in the Congo. Note how close the animals have come to human habitation. Will the Congolese continue this protection?

Below: Dr. Jacques Verschuren, one-time chief biologist of the Parc National Albert in the Congo, is now engaged in research in Serengeti. When political unrest brought chaos to the Congo, he continued to work for the interests of "le parc". He was arrested and beaten-up, but he continued to do all he could for his rangers and guides on a "grace and favour" basis. See Chapter 14.

SECTION FOUR

*

Congo

Between August and December, 1961, the author visited both Katanga and the Kivu Province in the Congo.

Independence for the Africans has brought many changes and some difficulties for men, like the European Dr. Verschuren and the African Bonaventure Mbula, who works for the preservation of the Parc National Albert.

Chapter 14

PYTHON JUNGLE

THE jokes of newspapermen friends to whom we had said that we would attempt to enter the Congo province of Kivu, which was then under the sway of the Stanleyville pro-Communist leader Anton Gizenga, had a distinctly ghoulish flavour. One recalled the occasion when he had sent a message, from the safety of Ruanda-Urundi, to Bakavu on the shores of Lake Kivu asking for permission to visit the town, and received the curt reply: "The first British reporter who sets foot in Kivu will be shot." Other's farewells were in the nature of "See you again some time—we hope."

All of the eleven letters which I had written a fortnight previously to black officials in Kivu Province and to the Leopoldville Central Government asking for authority to enter the Congo from Kisoro had remained unanswered. I had no visa or other entry papers. In Nairobi I had surrendered my old passport, which was studded with immigration stamps of the enemy Katanga State, and now possessed a brand new Kenya passport with blank pages. Before approaching the Congo border barrier I tore up my Katanga Press pass and United Nations *laisser passez*, both of which had been issued in Elizabethville, and scattered them among the banana trees.

I was jammed in the back of a station-wagon among small Belgian-type milk churns containing thirty-five gallons of petrol which had been obtained before leaving Kisoro. A scruffily-uniformed Congolese soldier at the border post beckoned to us to follow him into a sparsely furnished building where the African Immigration-cum-Customs officer waited behind his desk with an array of rubber stamps. There were several tense minutes and a general waving of arms. The Congolese District Commissioner, wearing a pin-stripe suit and maroon tie, arrived to join in the mêlée.

At the peak of a noisy deadlock my photographer companion had an inspiration. From his case he produced a Polaroid camera, posed the D.C. in the sunlight outside the border post and ten seconds later handed him a sharply-printed portrait photograph. Broad smiles and exclamations of surprise all round. The immigration official hurried off to fetch his wife and they were photographed together, followed by the beaming guard who stuck out his chest until the dirty brass buttons were at breaking-off point.

With the only formalities—a series of vigorous handshakes—over, we were on our way to our objectives. These were the famous two-million-acre Parc National Albert, which is situated at the bottom of the great African Rift between Lake Kivu in the first degree of latitude north on a stretch of some 200 miles, and a white man whose name had become a by-word for saving the Park single-handed in the midst of revolt, murder and cataclysm, when as he said: "The tribesmen wanted to kill all the animals and everyone said the Park was doomed."

This man was Dr. Jacques Verschuren, a bachelor in his middle thirties, who graduated in biology at the University of Louvain, and after working as a scientist in the field since 1948 (he once lived in a tent for two years at a stretch) ranks as the foremost Belgian authority in the field of African fauna. Our appointment was to meet him in his weathered villa in the old military post of Rutshuru.

When the Congo became independent, Dr. Verschuren stepped back as the Park's chief biologist, accepted an African boss and stayed on when other scientists and white wardens fled at the time of the revolt. Dr. Verschuren's friend, Walter Baumgartel, had told me: "He is a fanatic and a hero. The Congolese troops came and disarmed him. A few days later they gave him back his rifle. Then they returned, drunk, and wanted to shoot him. The muzzle of a rifle or a revolver was thrust into his mouth. When they let him go, he came to me. He did not run out of the Congo like thousands of his countrymen. True he went to Belgium and other parts of Europe, but to collect money and return to the Park to pay his scores of faithful African game rangers and guides who had received no money for months. On his return he was escorted back to his Rutshuru home by a patrol of United Nations soldiers, but Congolese troops arrived with in a matter of hours and arrested him—because they believed he had sold the Park to the United Nations! He was badly beaten up and again came to me, this time with all his scientific papers and photographs. One day, without hesitation or thought for his own safety, he went back to the Park because he had heard that his African staff had been attacked by soldiers from Stanleyville and he feared that the African *conservateur* with whom he had been arrested would be executed."

Dr. Verschuren proved to be tall, gangling, pale and highly-strung. He spoke French and broken English with machine-gun rapidity, and habitually wore sandals, shirt and the briefest of shorts. (See facing page 97.)

In Rutshuru petrol pumps were empty, cannibalized cars sagged on vacant lots and there were no cigarettes for sale in the stores—where indeed most of the shelves were empty even of goods usually regarded as necessities. We drew from the supplies of petrol we had brought in from Kisoro and drove in an ancient, groaning, lorry from Rutshuru to Rwindi, where the Park camp consisted of a large building used as a restaurant and bar and twenty-five new *rondavels*, well-equipped, with comfortable modern furniture, the latest types of plumbing and electric light. This was eerie luxury. The camp, modern and spotlessly clean and certainly one of the best to be found in Africa, was deserted. There was not a single tourist staying there.

Dr. Verschuren, whom the African staff of the Park still respectfully called "Patron", had no official position, received no salary, and operated on a delicate "grace and favour" basis, under which he was obliged to defer tactfully to the Congolese officials. So his first act on reaching the ghost camp of Rwindi was to pay his compliments to the African warden in charge, Monsieur

Bonaventure Mbula who, before his appointment following independence, was on the staff of the Information Department in Bukavu. M. Mbula, stocky and charming, who had achieved the average middle-class African's ambition of acquiring an office and a big desk covered with papers, seemed anxious to impress.

"Many people think Africans have no interest in game preservation, but that is not so here," he said briskly, as Dr. Verschuren remained in the background. "Of course, it is difficult in a new country like the Congo and we have to convince the people in the Government that our work is important." M. Mbula, who was appointed Warden of the Park after attending a conservation conference in Germany a year previously, was at pains to stress that his domain is "a strict nature preserve" and not a national park. But he continually referred to "le parc". He added: "We are very proud of the Park. I would like to keep it as it was created in 1935. The Park set an example then as a place where the animals could live in peace and where scientific research work went hand in hand with tourism, and I want it to continue to do so. We need as many tourists as possible coming here again. To that end some of my men are being trained to welcome them in English."

On a short trip the next day with Dr. Verschuren and M. Mbula we were joined by Monsieur Alain Gille, Unesco's Paris-based Science Officer for Africa, who was to report current conditions in the Park to his organization. I asked him why Unesco had done little to assist game conservation. M. Gille replied: "Unfortunately, there are so many countries and so many projects to help."

Walking towards the banks of the Rutshuru River, which has a hippo population of some 6,000, Dr. Verschuren explained that within the context of a "strict nature reserve" there was no cropping or any other interference with the life cycles of any of the animals. We inspected a barbed-wire enclosure within which there was tall grass, protected over the past two years, as compared with the bare, hippo-ravaged, land around. An elephant which had sun-baked, white legs after wading in the mud ambled by.

Sighting with his binoculars, Dr. Verschuren spotted the carcass and scattered bones of a 40-year-old elephant which, he said when we reached the spot, had died of natural causes two months before. The large tusks were still intact in the skull. "You see, no poaching here," exclaimed Dr. Verschuren proudly.

Back at the camp, the green-uniformed Congolese game rangers and guides, who had remained at their posts throughout the Congo's many turmoils, were drawn up on parade as the blue and gold-starred flag of the Republic fluttered above them. The men were addressed in French by M. Gille and M. Mbula, and the parade then marched past the two men at the salute, with Dr. Verschuren still remaining in the background. "I am certain now that the Park will survive—if only for prestige reasons," he whispered.

The stone monument to King Albert of the Belgians still stands undamaged in the Park near Rwindi Camp.

During another short tour of the Park before we returned temporarily to his home in Rutshuru, Dr. Verschuren took us to see a large colony of hippo in a small lake at the foot of towering peaks. A mud-covered beast resented the intrusion and, after opening its jaws widely in a menacing fashion, floundered out of the wallow and charged, its nostrils flaring red with rage. Dr. Verschuren coolly continued his discussion of the hippo culling programme, which he views with disfavour, in the Queen Elizabeth National Park. "There must be very, very many animals before there are too many," he said.

Dr. Verschuren then spent nine-tenths of the year in the bush, the jungle and on the mountains of the Park on scientific and anti-poaching foot *safaris* of the Livingstone style, now unusual in Africa. Many of his trips—some into dense, unexplored territory —last from ten days to three weeks with twenty or thirty African porters carrying the stores, tents and scientific and camping equipment in crates and bundles on their heads. Truculent and drunken Congolese soldiers had accused him of spying—for whom they were uncertain—on his *safaris*. He had managed to convince them on each occasion that his journeys were in the interests of peace, science and the Congolese themselves.

Stuffed specimens of rare small animals, snakes and rodents trapped by him on his expeditions are sent to Belgium to aid research work there. Dr. Verschuren had turned a room in his Rutshuru home into a well-equipped laboratory where he was assisted by two Africans.

He had agreed to take us on a short foot *safari*, and twenty porters, eager recruits from the town, filed on to the porch under the wing of his young head carrier, Isaac, for an armchair briefing by the biologist. The group was ringed by wide-eyed, ragged piccanins, some of whom Dr. Verschuren had helped to deliver in the absence of a midwife or medical doctor.

When the kit and food had been loaded on to the lorry, we piled in on top with the African porters, who having been presented with a group photograph taken by the Polaroid, chanted happily in Kiswahili as we lurched along "The magic eye will protect us". I found myself wishing I could share their faith, for I had noticed that no member of the party, not even an African game ranger of the Park staff who was laboriously trying to master a few guide-book phrases of English, carried any firearm. Dr. Verschuren, still in his short shorts and shirt, displayed nothing more lethal than a small pair of binoculars strung round his neck.

When we were within sight of a patch of jungle on the horizon after a two-hour drive, Dr. Verschuren brought the lorry to a jerking, smoking halt—briskly announcing the start of the trail and a burnt-out clutch. He strode off at the head of his crocodile of porters, setting a herd of buffalo scampering and "flushing" a four-foot-long dragon-like lizard from the reeds of a pool.

"A good omen, *bwana*," muttered one of the porters. "The *patron* once saved one of them from the jaws of a python, and the lizards are now his guardians." At that moment he rolled his eyes in fear, flung the camp stools on his head to the ground and scattered with the rest of the porters. A hippo had stumbled out of the pool and was thundering towards us. Dr. Verschuren calmly stood his ground yelling "Stoopid 'ippo" until the infuriated animal veered away and the trembling porters resumed the trek.

Pangas, or machetes, were used to hack a path through the jungle—infested said Dr. Verschuren, with pythons, cobras, puff adders and scorpions—to a clearing where we pitched camp for the night amid thousands of pelicans and their fledglings nesting in the candelabra of the tall euphorbia trees.

Having bandaged the leg of an injured African porter (he himself justifiably claimed to have acquired a leather skin on which no cuts or scratches appeared), Dr. Verschuren warned me: "If you are trampled on by an elephant or a hippo in your tent tonight, it's not the Park's responsibility." We left the camp together to take twilight tape recordings in "Python Jungle" of the symphony of sounds—baby pelicans in chorus low like a herd of cows—and to collect specimens of insects, plants, earth, water and vegetation.

Dr. Verschuren has the reputation of knowing every type of animal, bird, reptile and insect in the Park.

We had walked beyond sight and sound of the camp in the gloom when he beckoned me to squat on the ground and disappeared after struggling into the heart of a clump of bushes with his recorder. I had been warned to make no sound, and for half an hour I crouched, uncomfortably and silently, sweeping away legions of ants attacking my legs and arms, until a shout of "Bon" from le docteur ended the ordeal and, guided by the firelight, we stumbled over roots and past cruel thorn bushes to the camp.

His African cook had prepared an excellent dinner of soup, a stew with mushrooms, apple "fool" and coffee, which we ate at a metal table by the light of a hurricane lamp, bombarded by moths and mosquitoes, while lion, hippo and elephant roared and squealed around us. New logs had been tossed on the fire and my bedroll in the small, green tent allocated to me was being searched for poisonous snakes as Dr. Verschuren, munching ginger nuts, leaned back and flipped the pages of an illustrated book on the Congo's birds and flowers.

He combined the qualified statements of the scientist with a guarded reserve of expression necessitated by his tightrope position between the possibility of being ordered out of the Congo by U.N. as a Belgian and continuing to be allowed to serve in the Park by the erratic goodwill of the Congolese. Here, however, among the surroundings he loved so deeply and fervently, as moonlight cast grotesque shadows, he was in a mood to talk freely.

"Mon Dieu, the United Nations, it seems, is prepared to spend ten million dollars on some Egyptian temple when only a tenth of that money would serve all the national parks in Africa," he said with the bitterness of a man struggling against the indifference of the outside world and African primitiveness. "We have not had a penny from the U.N.; and a dollar today is worth 100 dollars in two years' time."

Dr. Verschuren claims there is less poaching in the Parc National Albert than any other on the African Continent, and he is intensely proud of the fact that the Park's game rangers and guides, although very poorly paid in contrast to the Congolese soldiers, have remained keen, efficient, and well-disciplined. Poaching in the Park, he said, was generally carried out by bands of tribesmen who came over from Uganda, armed with spears and bows and poisoned arrows.

He told of a pitched battle ten miles inside the Park between twenty-five poachers and seven of the Congolese game guards, armed only with spears, who finally drove off the savage intruders after one of the guards had been killed and mutilated and another critically wounded. When Dr. Verschuren found the wounded man under a tree, the first question the victim gasped was: "Did they kill any of the animals?"

His eyes were moist as he stared into the embers of the camp-fire. "What greater proof could I ask of these Africans' concern for the Park and its creatures?"

One fear Dr. Verschuren has is that the guards in the field may be tempted to spend most of their duty hours at their posts, confining any patrols they made to the roads, for reasons of personal prestige among their fellow Africans. He was concerned, too, about the pygmy hunters in the equatorial forest of the northern tip of the Park. These men are experts in tracking down and killing elephant and other big game with tiny bows and poison-tipped arrows.

"They are killing lots of animals with snares alone," he said. "And they are allowed to continue because the authorities regard the pygmies as part of the *fauna* of the region."

The half-moon was high in the sky by the time we went to bed. With only a thin sheet of green canvas between me and the the beasts of "Python Jungle", every snapping twig set my nerves jangling, but I fell asleep at last. . . . A shattering ripping of branches and a shout from Dr. Verschuren awoke me. I dived under the laced flaps of the tent. It was ten minutes past midnight, and fifteen feet away from my tent a bull elephant was on the rampage. He looked a ghostly mass in the moon-glow.

Barefoot and in his pyjamas, Dr. Verschuren advanced yelling: "Tembo 'way . . . Tembo 'way." That seemed to scare him off but within a matter of minutes the fearsome intruder was back. By then Dr. Verschuren had extracted a small-calibre revolver from the bottom of one of his tin trunks and, as we swept the trees with the beams of our electric torches, he fired into the air two shots that scared off the animal for the night.

Dr. Verschuren, up at first light to make recordings of baboons barking, forgot the elephant incident in the excitement of playing back his tape on which he had recorded the clear "*ba*-boon" cries from which, it seems, these animals derive their name.

After our breakfast of paw-paw, salami and cream cheese, we broke camp and returned to Rutshuru in a "relief" lorry which had the distinction of travelling one kilometre to every gallon of water. We proceeded, however, at a spanking pace; our ruffianly, good-natured porters, pelican feathers stuck in the peppercorns of their hair, urged us to join in their tribal songs and, with a boisterous, child-like abandon, shouted endearments and obscenities to the Congolese women whom we passed on the road.

From his own pocket, Dr. Verschuren paid the porters their 2s. a day, and had given his household staff three-quarters of their weekly wages when the middle-aged garden "boy" approached him in the lounge of the villa and took off his cap. With respectful sadness, he explained that he would have to have his full money because a young child was sick. The selfless scientist replied gently that he was giving them all the money he had, and his own at that.

"Pardon, *patron*," said the man. "Then I shall have to write to the King of the Belgians."

The dubious blessings of fifteen months of independence, with all its fulsome flag-wagging and waves of freedom propaganda, had passed him by.

[Since this chapter was written Dr. Verschuren has become engaged in a number of research projects in Serengeti.]

*

Rhodesia

Northern and Southern

The area was visited by the author between October, 1961 and May, 1962.

Here he deals with fire as an adjunct to hunting; animal rescue; game farming and its economic potentials and a children's game that teaches conservation.

Chapter 15

FIERY SLAUGHTER

IN the middle reaches of its 1,000-mile course from the Congo to the Zambezi, the Kafue River flows slowly and coolly between the thick growth of reeds bordering its main channel. Because of its slowness, the silt which it claims from the eroded soil of its catchment area sinks gently to the bottom, leaving the water clear and clean.

Scattered along the river's banks are occasional clusters of rudely-built grass-and-reed shelters, where local fishermen establish themselves transiently for the fishing season, and from whence they set out in their clumsy dug-out canoes to net the *tilapia* in which the river abounds. At dust, spirals of smoke mark the dung fires over which the fish are cured before being taken in trucks or on bicycles over rough hippopotamus-pocked tracks to the urban centres of population 200 miles distant.

Across the great plain which flanks the river, in the park-like bushline which marks its limits, stand the more permanent villages some of which retain the traditional horse-shoe design of ancient times, with a stockaded cattle pen in the centre and the preserve of the chief and his wives (even more strongly stockaded against intruders) at one end. The huts, with their brightly daubed mud walls, neat *stoeps* and tidy thatch topped by decorative antelope horns make gay patches amongst the wild fig and flaring "lucky-bean" trees. Children, wearing little charms and bracelets and nothing else, caper amongst the paw-paw and banana trees; skinny dogs, with metal discs strung around their necks to record their inoculation against rabies, pant in the shade of the huts; women pound maize, prepare relishes, brew beer or suckle their babies; the younger men, those who have not gone to find work in the mines or on the farms of the European areas, tend the cattle or prepare their lands for the crop-growing season. The older men, those who have returned from seeking their fortunes, sit by their huts or beneath the trees, talking. Sometimes the village will boast a tractor, symbol of its transition from tribalism towards capitalism.

In such villages live the people of the Ila tribe, a race whose origins go back into the uncharted times of Northern Rhodesia's history, and whose claim to have been the first tribe on the Kafue is supported by customs and characteristics which set them apart from the other Bantu groups—the Matabele, the Lozi, the Makololo and Barotse—who marauded and settled in the area during the latter half of the nineteenth century, before the coming of the *Pax Britannica*.

Today the Ila proper are few in number, although their blood and influence have extended to many associated or mixed tribes —Mbwela, Lundwe, Lumbu, Sala and Ila-Tonga—covering a vast area from the Lukanga swamps to the Zambezi River. One of the reasons for the small population of pure Ila is the tribal custom of *lumbabo* which, by its acceptance of polyandry, has led to a devastating spread of venereal disease.

Others of their customs, such as the wearing of the *isusu*, a coiffure of mud and hair, up to four feet tall, built on the head and rising to a sharp point, (a device designed to enable hunting parties to see each other above the grass of the plains), have long since fallen out of use. Others still, like the knocking out of four or six of the upper front teeth, (a custom believed to originate from a desire by the tribesmen to resemble their cattle), are no longer practised. Indeed, some of the older men, in their urge to be dissociated from the past have restored their broad smiles with false teeth.

Although time and new ideas have worked on the people, slowly adjusting them from a warrior-tribe to a pastoral existence, some of the traditions continue. Among those which have survived all change is the annual buffalo drive when the Baila— the tribesmen of the Ila—match their spears and skill against

Above: This bush fire was started by the hand of man. The sweeping flames help Baila tribesmen to drive buffalo to a "killing ground" where, with their thin and fragile-looking spears, the animals are slain. The fire itself cannot be checked and sweeps on, long after it has served the Bailas' turn, destroying pasture and the habitats of game until some natural firebreak such as a river or rocky outcrop, robs it of fuel. For a short-term advantage the Baila destroy each year countless square miles of habitat for game.

Below: Baila tribesmen at the kill; a hitherto unpublished photograph.

Above: All too often to the African the slaying of an elephant is a matter for celebration. Ivory to sell; meat to eat: these are the immediate gains. That indiscriminate killing means eventual extinction for the animal is beyond the comprehension of people who live only for today. Only slowly is the idea that preservation of wild game is in their own interest gaining any widespread acceptance among the tribes.

Left: All too seldom can the slayers of game be surprised and caught in the act. All too often the primitive but effective methods of resident Africans are supplemented by raids from far afield staged with the help of motor vehicles and rifles which on occasions are used to resist arrest.

one of Africa's strongest and, when wounded, most dangerous animals.

Although the origin of this custom is unknown, the two major influences in its development—factors which, at one time or another, have moulded the traditions of many African peoples—could well have been the need for meat and the desire to test the manhood of the tribe. Whatever its beginnings, the annual Baila buffalo drive has survived unaltered to this time, and, in surviving, provides a rare glimpse into Africa's past.

Towards the end of the dry season, when the air is heavy with dust and smoke, and the ground is baked hard and dry from months of exposure to the probing heat of the sun, the marshes which flank the Kafue River have seeped or evaporated away, leaving only residual lagoons, slimy and stagnant, and limitless expanses of parched, grass-covered flats.

Here, with herds of zebra and antelope, driven from the parched bush in search of grazing and water, the buffalo collect. Sometimes, if the previous rainy season has been a poor one, they will gather on the plains in their thousands; at other times, when heavy rains have left lingering moisture over wide areas late into the dry season, the buffalo may number only two or three hundred. As they graze over the plains their movements are watched by the Baila, casually rather than methodically, for the game always congregates in the same area and the tribesmen's main interest is in its numbers.

The weather, too, is watched. The drive must be carried out as late in the dry season as possible to enable the hunters to compensate their sparseness on the ground by the employment of an ally, fire. Yet the drive must not be so late that the first showers of the new rains have dampened the grass or turned the plains once again into marshes. When the probabilities are agreed a day is set for the drive, and what few preparations are needed—the sharpening of a spear head, or the renewal of a haft—are undertaken.

At Namwala, the district's centre, which comprises a few groups of offices, houses and Indian-owned stores scattered in a spur of the bushline which here intrudes across the plain to the very edge of the Kafue River, those whose duty will take them as observers to the drive, which is held under the authority of the chief, also make their few preparations—the cleaning of a rifle or the packing of a lunch basket. From this calm and remote settlement, with a European population of a few families, vast stretches of Northern Rhodesia are administered and developed, and from here the district's officers set out on the appointed day to the buffalo drive.

Before the sun has risen, and while the air is still clear from its overnight cleansing from the dew, two parties leave the Boma in their Land-Rovers. The first heads west along the south bank of the river. The second travels due east for a few miles and then crosses the river on a hand-winched pontoon. From there it doubles back along the north bank, passes through a gate in a tsetse-fly control fence and takes up position in the bushline overlooking the great plains. In the meanwhile the first party has abandoned its Land-Rover on the south bank, crossed the river in a dug-out-canoe, and taken up a vantage point on an ant-hill near the river's edge. Both parties are now positioned at opposite extremities of the flats with some three and a half miles separating them. Between lies the lagoon-studded, undulating Iyezha Plain where the drive is to take place.

As the heat increases and the first gusts of wind begin to charge the air with its daily burden of dust, the tribesmen move out from their villages in knots of two or three or more to muster on the perimeter of the plain. Most of them are either very young or in the years of middle age. They wear tattered singlets and shorts, or just loincloths, and carry unornamented eight-foot spears, flimsy yet beautifully balanced. With them they bring their dogs, a motley collection of beasts displaying an astonishing range of breeding permutations, from the lion dog, with its reversed ridge of hair along the spine, to the animal which reveals an ancestry in which Alsatian, Airedale, Black Labrador and wild dog may all have played their part.

By nine o'clock up to 200 Baila are scattered in groups on either side of the Iyezha. On the southern extremity a herd of 300 buffalo, almost hidden by the mounting haze and the undulations of the ground, grazes unconcerned. To the east, a column of smoke rises as a party of men set fire to the grass between the bush-line and the river. Their purpose is to isolate the Iyezha section from the remainder of the plain and prevent the escape of any buffalo. Another column of smoke to the west marks a parallel attempt to create a barrier on that side, and this is soon followed by a third fire to the north, between the bushline and the plain. The southern edge, already barred by the river, is left unfired.

As the flames gather in strength the geometrical intention loses its shape and system. Patches of moisture, stretches of water and gusts of wind combine to re-form the pattern of the fire into an uncontrolled blaze, creeping in one place, halting in another, spurting in **wild** dashes in others. (See facing page 112.)

Soon, burning inwards and outwards, accelerated by the wind which its own heat engenders, forming a jigsaw of black and brown patches, the fire extends over thousands of acres. The columns of smoke marking the first burnings having merged into one slanting pillar which, through some chemical action on the atmosphere, culminates in a great cumulus cloud hanging heavily in the sky.

On the ground the sweeping winds gather up the ash and smoke, driving them across and smothering the plains. Groups of Baila appear, briefly silhouetted against the smoky background as they advance, not with the military discipline of extended order, but patchily and without cohesion. Instinctively, alert and watch-ful for any break-out, they head for the now invisible centre of the Iyezha where they expect to find the buffalo.

The animals grow increasingly restive and disturbed, but soon they are obscured from view by the growing pall of smoke. From the bushline, awaiting the opportunity to move on to the plain, the observers watch the developing conflagration. To their left, 200 yards away, a herd of zebra breaks out of the bush, chased by a pack of dogs, and charges across the grass towards the curtain of smoke. The animals check, wheel and stampede in a tightly packed mass. After blindly circling at top speed, they head back into the bushline leaving only a trail of panting dogs and a thick cloud of dust to mark their panic-stricken course.

As the morning advances, and the sun's light is dimmed, while its heat seems magnified by the widening haze of smoke, other animals appear from time to time; first a pair of reedbuck, then a few puku, then another reedbuck calmly grazing on the verge of the fire. Birds drift overhead waiting the chance to swoop and snatch the harvest of insects driven before the flames. The Baila spearmen have long since disappeared into the murk and, except for the steady sound of the wind blowing over the flats and the distant thunder of the fire, all is quiet.

African boma messengers are summoned from the shade of a fig tree, rifles are loaded (nothing in the breech is a necessary precaution against the jolting of the Land-Rover) and they set off across the open ground towards the first lagoon half a mile away. They drive along the edge of the lagoon, bumping and jerking over a maze of hippo spoor baked deep into the ground, until a likely fording place is reached. Here the water narrows to a few yards with a thick, matted covering of weeds on its far side. The Africans test the depth and the feeling of the underlying mud. Some take their boots off, others don't bother, but all are soon floundering in three feet of water and foul-smelling slime. They search for more solid places but usually without success. So, they stand in a chain across the ford, ready to put their shoulders to the Land-Rover if it should start to slip.

One of the Europeans, his clothes dripping and glutinous, reverses the car into a take-off position. In low-ratio gear he drives steadily into the lagoon, throwing up a sheet of spray as the chassis hits the water. The car grinds smoothly through, mounts the edge of the mat of weeds, advances, checks, and sinks slowly into the slime, its wheels churning angrily and impotently.

The Africans plunge towards it, slipping and sliding as their feet try to grip the bottom. Together they put their shoulders behind the vehicle. As they push and heave, the climax of the drive has

approached on the southern extremity of the Iyezha, three miles
away. Here two men standing on an ant-hill, are alert for any
sign of the herd which disappeared from view hours before.
Visibility has decreased even further and the sound of crackling
grass, now burning patchily in several places close by, prevents
them from hearing the buffalo. On other ant-hills discernible
through the smoke, groups of Baila stand with their spears, looking like martial statues.

Someone shouts "*bunyati*" and, quite suddenly, the buffalo
appear charging directly towards the two men on their ant-hill
There are about 160 of them and they stampede straight across
the open flat. Their hooves beat down the grass and churn the
hard-baked soil into a powdery dust which floats away to mingle
with the driving smoke.

The herd starts breaking up and rushes past on either side of the
ant-hill, its steep sides acting as a breakwater to the advancing
tide.

The buffalo, now checked by a small lagoon, worried by the
dogs and confused by the increasing noise of the spearmen as they
leave their ant-hills and dash in, disintegrate as a herd and scatter
in many directions. Some blunder across the lagoon or crash into
a nearby solitary patch of trees, others charge wildly through the
smouldering fires on to the scorched plains beyond. Yet others,
milling wildly around, are marked down by the spearmen and
their dogs. One young beast buffets five mongrels mercilessly as
they snarl and tear at its flanks. Then it leaps away, flailing its
assailants with heavy hooves. A spear flies straight and fast and the
animal falls, killed outright. Other buffalo meet the same end and
the massive shapes, weighing as much as a ton, crash to the ground
impaled by the thin, fragile spears of the Baila.

In the murk and confusion of the mêlée most of the beasts
escape, either on to the smouldering plain or into the lagoons
where they take refuge, standing rigid and still in the water, concealed by the fringe of reeds. The dogs are not sent to smell them
out for, in the past, too many have been taken by crocodiles.

Instead, any spearmen who are not already preoccupied in examining and discussing the kills, concentrate on the buffalo now dashing in scattered groups towards the bushline. Other huntsmen, those who have been advancing across the plain from the bushline, partly cut off the buffaloes' line of retreat, but, in the ever-mounting haze of dust and ash and smoke, little can be seen of their quarry.

The Land-Rover, now extricated from the sludge of the lagoon, also heads towards the escaping buffalo but its occupants are unaware that the animals have broken out from the centre of the plain. As they drive across the blackened ground, clouds of powdered ash billow over and into the car, adding to the dirt and mud already collected from the lagoon. The vehicle makes wide detours to avoid patches of flaming grass, and pauses occasionally, as the smoke momentarily lifts, to check on the direction. After a while a fluttering movement in the distance is spotted which, as the car approaches, is seen to be the heavy-winged flapping of vultures as they circle and squabble round the carcass of a dead buffalo. As the car stops the birds lumber off leaving great patches of droppings trickling off the animal's hide. Amongst them as they flop and hop lazily around is another of Africa's scavengers, a lone marabou stork.

The buffalo has been killed by a spear wound in the neck and has fallen in this spot after a solitary death rush from the scene of the main battle. It is a 3-year-old, weighing about a ton, and already it is swollen and distorted by its own degenerative heat. Its hide is blistered and scorched and around it the plain is charred by fire, but beneath its body the grass is unburnt, showing that it has fallen and died mercifully before the flames passed over it.

Two young buffalo rush across an open patch towards a group of spearmen, who run to cut them off. But the animals swerve and are soon lost to view, leaving their hunters to wallow fruitlessly in a patch of soft ground. The dogs have not spotted the two beasts and their scent is confused by the heavy smell of the burning grass.

Farther on, as the Land-Rover nears the southern party, three great bulls lumber out of the smoke, their shapes enormous against the murky background. They stand looking at the car, their noses thrown up and their horns lying back against their shoulders. A snow-white egret rises from the back of one, circles for a few moments and alights again to resume its search on the buffalo's hide. The animals turn and walk slowly away along the line of smoke until they, too, disappear.

Tribesmen are either clustered around their kills or standing on their ant-hills alert for any new sign of game.

One Land-Rover party making a crossing of the river finds itself in a dry spot hemmed on the far side by a thin line of fire. Driving through this, they find themselves in the centre of a small ring of fire. The driver turns the wheel hard and the Land-Rover breaks out again, leaning precariously as it bumps along the slope of a lagoon. Once clear of the fire a stop is made to look under the body; since no burning grass is caught upon the chassis they drive on to join the southern group.

When they arrive the butchering is far advanced and little that is recognizable is left of the animal. Dogs snap and snarl on the outskirts as they wait for the scraps that are thrown to them. The men themselves hack at the carcase or perform mock war dances to show their glee. The smell is strong. There is no arguing as to possession, nor as to who shall have which parts of the meat.

Elsewhere on the plain other groups are performing the same task. Altogether the hunters have killed ten buffalo. Among the spearmen there are no casualties, but some of the dogs are bruised or limping. Few of the escaped buffalo are thought to be wounded or burnt and this gives the game officers much satisfaction.

Beyond the lagoon the hunt continues, desultorily, as small groups of spearmen try to track down animals from the scattered herd. But little can be seen and gradually the hunters give up their quest and collect round the kills to gossip and help in the butchering. Some stragglers are told of an unclaimed kill and they move off eagerly to collect it. When they arrive, some four hours after the animal was first seen, the vultures and the marabou are still

there and have not yet succeeded in breaking into the tough hide
—or perhaps they are waiting for the bigger scavengers, the hyena
and jackal, to do their work, leaving the inner flesh exposed.

Soon the Baila begin to load their gruesome prizes upon their
shoulders. Some of the meat will be eaten fresh that evening,
grilled by the women over bright fires, while the men drink beer
and re-live the adventures of the day; the rest will be dried in the
sun to make biltong for the weeks ahead.

As the spearmen make their way in cheerful groups towards
their villages, the fire continues to spread and smoulder across the
plain. The sun, now well beyond its zenith, is visible as a yellow
glare, blurred and filtered by the heavy layer of smoke and dust.
It casts no shadows and the earth is diffused with a uniform brassy
glow. The heat is unabated and the wind blows in hot gusts,
spiralling occasionally into furious dust-devils which spin and
roar across the ground, sucking great quantities of ash and frag-
ments of scorched grass into the sky where they hang in thick
funnels, scattering the vultures.

Though the hunting had ended the fires started by the hunters
blazed on unchecked—as do hundreds of others which are started
every year, heedless of eventual consequences, and not always only
by uneducated tribesmen. These fires rage through vast stretches
of sparsely populated terrain until their progress is checked by
some natural firebreak such as a lake or river, rocky terrain or
already burnt-off area, or perhaps by a man-made obstacle in the
form of ploughed land, a dirt road or railway track, or perhaps
one of the very few forest clearings which have been made to stem
the roaring fury of the bush fire.

Creeping down mountainsides, turning valleys into "rivers"
of smoky red and eventually leaving valley and *veld* alike a
blackened desolation, these bush fires started by primitive peoples
deep inside bushland or jungle, are all too often a part of the
African scene in the dry season. For it is beyond the comprehension of the tribesmen to take precautions against a holocaust which
can destroy not only the vegetation but the animals around them,

Above: Gertie the most-photographed wild animal in the world. For details of her magnificent horn see pages 22 and 25.

Below: Drought is the most terrible, and hardest to combat, of all the dangers facing Africa's big game. Here a rhinoceros digs deeply but unsuccessfully for life-sustaining water.

Top, left: These darts, which can be fired from a rifle or a specially-constructed crossbow, are hypodermic syringes through which a paralysing drug can be administered. *Top, right:* Once the hypodermic dart has struck the animals must be followed swiftly, for unless an antidote is administered, the drugged animal may die.

Below: Though the dart still sticks into its shoulder the rhino is lively; the men who have lassoed its legs are still a long way from its capture.

Above: The antidote is taking effect: until it is certain that the ropes will hold, a strong grip to keep down the rhino's head and so prevent it from rising, is a wise measure.

Right: Once the rhino is immobilized the heavy work of loading it for transport to an animal sanctuary can be undertaken.

Above: Rupert Fothergill was the senior game warden in charge of the rescue operations on Lake Kariba (see Chapter 16). When this rhino attacked, he hit it with his bush hat.

Below: On releasing the rhino in its new home the rangers daringly give its tail a valedictory pull.

so being a threat to the very existence of themselves and their families. The ranks of those with greater knowledge and experience are thin—far too thin on the ground as yet to be able to minimize the annual destruction of life and vegetation which can render the bleak livelihood of the native tribes more meagre than need be.

Chapter 16

RHINO ON A RAFT

" We spent a day with the Southern Rhodesian animal rescue team, and can testify to the adventurous nature of the proceedings and the zeal and gallantry with which they were carried out. There has been some criticism of the operation on the grounds that the rescued animals would be transported to areas already well stocked with wild life, and so would be unlikely to maintain themselves permanently : and that the large amount of money and skilled manpower employed would have been better expended on more constructive conservation projects. I do not agree. In the first place, to leave this assemblage of strange and beautiful creatures to drown was unthinkable, and would have provoked a formidable world outcry. And, on the positive side, it has helped the general public of the civilized world to realize both the unique richness of African wild life and the dangers with which it is threatened." Prof. Julian Huxley in his report on a mission undertaken for Unesco on "The Conservation of Wild Life and Natural Habitats in Central and East Africa".

WHEN Rupert Fothergill, 49-year-old senior game ranger in charge of the "Operation Noah" rescue operations on Lake Kariba in British Central Africa, announced that he would have a go at saving the larger animals—rhinoceros and elephant—marooned on islands created by the floodwaters of the Zambezi, eyebrows were raised in scepticism.

As one who had previously watched the rangers engaged in a task that has captured the imagination of people all over the world

through the media of books, newspaper articles, cinema and television screens, I shared the doubts. True, I had seen Fothergill and
his team perform the most astonishing feats.

Men who will wrestle bare-handed in shallow water with
frenzied baboons and fully-grown porcupines, lasso and tether
swimming giant buck, clad only in swimming trunks climb trees
to capture deadly black mambas, are obviously capable of almost
anything. But it would require something more than superlative
courage and resource to rescue the huge pachyderms from death
by drowning or starvation. How could these enormous, ferocious
brutes be caught and rendered helpless on their shrinking island
homes, then conveyed across stretches of water sometimes several
miles wide, and finally set free on the mainland?

Fothergill pondered the problem for a long time. Eventually he
found the solution. It was one that enlisted the aid of science to
supplement the skill and daring of the puny humans engaged in
the task.

I was fortunate enough to be a member of a party that watched
a rhino rescue and an abortive, but nonetheless exciting attempt
to save an elephant. For sheer, blood-tingling thrills, it surpassed
any experience that had come my way on *safari*. Both rhino and
elephant behaved in a way that would have gladdened any Hollywood mogul's heart. If our quarry had been trained to act a part
they could not have been more co-operative.

Archie Fraser, head of Southern Rhodesia's Wild Life Conservation Department, warned us before we set out that it was by no
means certain that we should see what we had come to see; the
reaction of the "big chaps" to a hunt was always unpredictable.
At the end of two days, however, we fully endorsed the sentiment
expressed by Southern Rhodesia's Minister of Lands, Reuben
Stumbles, that we had taken part in an expedition that any wealthy
safari-loving tourist would have paid a fortune to have accompanied.

Our venue on the first day was an island about three miles long
and half a mile wide on which a 2,000 lb. female rhino was living.

The only other occupants were a leopard and a few kudu and impala. On the trip from the base camp at Kariba in the launch (suitably named *The Ark*) and accompanied by a little flotilla of three fast motor-boats, Fothergill explained the techniques employed in rhino- and elephant-rescues.

A ranger fires a dart containing a carefully calculated dose of a "knockout" drug from a rifle into the animal's hide. The rhino gallops away, but about fifteen to thirty minutes after being hit it drops to the ground insensible. The rangers then rope its legs together so that it cannot get to its feet. An antidote to the drug is immediately injected—the drug dosage would otherwise almost certainly kill the beast—and a tranquillizing drug is administered at the same time. The trussed rhino is heaved on to an improvised sledge and hauled on to a raft made buoyant with empty petrol drums and tractor-tyre inner tubes. The raft is towed to the mainland by a motor-boat.

Once the sledge has been dragged back on to dry land, the rangers untie the ropes—and stand well back. The rhino at this stage is conscious, but generally does not get to his feet until Rupert Fothergill flings a couple of buckets of water over it. As the rhino rises, Rupert runs for his life. The rhino invariably charges the first person or object it sees as it regains its feet.

A fully-grown elephant is too bulky to be manhandled on to a sledge, so the rangers drive it into the water by shouting, banging cans and the firing of rifles and Verey-pistol cartridges. The elephant is an excellent swimmer and will often make its own way to the mainland. Where the stretch of water is too great for its swimming capacities, the rescue team tows it by a rope thrown as a lasso over its head.

Even Fothergill's matter-of-fact tone as he outlined these procedures could not conceal the exciting potentialities of our trip. What we actually saw happen exceeded our highest hopes.

On arriving at Rhino Island, we were directed to a vantage point on a tree-lined height while Fothergill stalked his prey. Archie Fraser strictly forbade any of the spectators to accompany

Fothergill, not only because of the grave danger, but because a carelessly trampled stick or even the rustle of leaves could easily startle the rhino—an animal with extremely sensitive hearing— and scare it away before the ranger got in his shot.

Eventually African scouts reported that a rhino had made her way to a smaller island, only a few square yards in area, separated from the main one by a narrow strip of easily-fordable water.

So we shinned up trees and waited while two rangers took a boat to the far side of the rhino's new island refuge and, by shouting and banging cans, panicked her into rushing into the shallows. Sending up tremendous showers of spray, the rhino failed to see Fothergill, rifle at the ready, lurking behind a tree in the ford itself. The ranger shot his dart into her shoulder from two yards range as she plunged past him.

From my vantage point in the branches of a *mopani* sapling, about twelve feet from the ground, I suddenly saw a ton of enraged rhinoceros galloping full tilt at my perilous perch. As she approached it seemed impossible that she could manoeuvre her massive bulk past the tree, and I had a momentary horrifying vision of the slender trunk snapping like a match-stick and hurling me into her path. But, with a margin of a split second left, she swerved. As the tree shook violently from the impact of her flank, I looked down, clinging frantically to a branch, on to her back and saw her sinister curved horns pass just under my feet.

Fothergill streaked after her into the bush.

Half an hour later we heard Fothergill's whistled signal, repeated at intervals until we traced its source after running almost a mile across the island.

When we arrived, Fothergill and his helpers had trussed the rhino where she lay prostrate at the spot where she had succumbed to the drug. When the antidote was administered, the beast became frenzied, in spite of the injection of a tranquillizer. Repeatedly she bashed her head against the ground, damaging herself against rocks. She plunged her scimitar-shaped horns into a tree trunk. When a ranger tried to prevent her from injuring herself by

placing a straw-filled sack behind her head she twisted her neck
and sent it hurtling thirty feet through the air.

The rangers and scouts had an almost superhuman tussle to haul
the rhino on to the sledge. At one stage, in spite of the shackling
ropes, she almost got to her feet and men, white and black, went
hurtling in various directions. Eventually, however, the task was
completed and the rhino was towed on the raft to the mainland.

There, she became even more angry. In her struggles while
being released, her head became pointed towards the shore. By the
time she had regained her feet, Fothergill, who had stood a couple
of yards from her, sluicing her huge body with water from a pail,
had taken refuge on the raft, moored a few yards from the shore.
The first object the rhino spotted was one of the motor-boats, also
moored in the shallows a short distance from the raft. Head down,
she charged straight at it.

Some of my companions and I had chosen the boat deck as a
platform from which to watch the final stages of the rescue. We
instantly regretted it, for the brute hit the boat with the impact of
a tank, hurling us backwards into the well. As we picked ourselves
up, jarred and shaken, she plunged her horn three times into the
boat's hull, making holes through the metal the size of a man's
fist just above the waterline.

Then the rhino caught sight of Fothergill standing on the raft.
At once she plunged through the water and stood alongside it,
lunging at him repeatedly with her horn. Nonchalantly, Rupert
stood his ground and calmly removing his bush-hat slapped the
beast with it several times across the face. It was a superb example
of cool nerve—almost as if it had been rehearsed. Spontaneously
we burst into a round of clapping, and then, seeing that this
distracted the rhino, began to shout at the top of our voices. She
turned and took off in a bull-dozing gallop into the bush.

We set off from Kariba the next day for a more distant island—
a mere strip of land thirty yards long by ten wide, where a great
bull elephant had made his temporary home.

The plan was to drive him into the water, give him a "shot" of knockout drug while he was swimming, then lasso and revive him so that he could make his own way to the mainland, half-a-mile distant.

This was a plan that went astray. With incredible cunning, our quarry managed to elude the rangers every time and return to his strip of ground above water-level. Eventually he was driven into fairly deep water and at one stage was actually swimming. *The Ark* manoeuvred alongside and a ranger threw a lariat. He missed. Four times the enraged beast drove his tusks into the boat's hull, leaving deep dents that almost penetrated the quarter-inch metal. Then he found the shallows again and clambered back on to his island strip.

We had to leave him there for another rescue attempt—another day.

By the end of 1961 a total of 3,685 animals, 402 reptiles and 52 birds had been rescued from the Southern Rhodesian half of Lake Kariba since the giant dam wall across the Zambezi was plugged in December, 1958. Of this total 17 elephant had been saved, 19 rhino, 288 bushbuck, 13 buffalo, 1,270 impala, 182 kudu, 477 warthog, 45 zebra, 10 night apes, 4 scaly ant-eaters, 169 monkeys, 5 squirrels, a black-footed domestic cat left behind in a doomed village by tribesmen, 32 porcupines, 36 antbears and many other species of game.

I returned to Kariba in June, 1962. That bull elephant had long since dog-padded to the mainland, but, with the lake rising rapidly, Rupert and his men were hard at work, from dawn to darkness, seven days a week. On one dying island alone there were then estimated to be over 100 elephant, which swam to and from the nearby "coast", and an equal number of buffalo. Five hundred impala were trapped on another island.

Rupert, who had had a six-weeks-old orphan rhino he had saved named after him by a Salisbury family which adopted it, mentioned in passing that his five broken ribs had mended. I had heard nothing about his injuries. They arose from yet another encounter with a rhino. He had taken refuge behind a tree when a fully-grown rhino charged, but the tree had been eaten through by soldier ants and collapsed under the onslaught. Spreadeagled, Rupert was pinned beneath the kneeling, panting animal yet, after what seemed the final, searing moments of his job, he was able to wriggle clear between its hind legs and was dragged away by his helpers.

Drinking morning tea at the Kariba base camp, I remarked that there had been no lion rescues throughout the years of "Operation Noah". There was a twinkle in his eyes and his leathery features cracked into a grin that for him was almost smug as Rupert took my arm. "Let's go," he said. "I want to show you a secret."

During the seven-mile trip in *The Ark* from Kariba to an island two miles long and a few hundred yards wide Rupert gave no clue as to the purpose of our mystery expedition, and when we had landed, followed by two African game scouts with rifles, he merely glanced over his shoulder and remarked: "We'll take a stroll."

The stroll, a strenuous march with thorns ripping my bush-shirt, lasted two hours and in that time we criss-crossed the brooding island. Vultures led us to a stinking buffalo carcass. With every rustle in the thick undergrowth, the gun-bearers stiffened. Rupert "froze", crouched, then shook his head and smiled as a wart hog scampered off. He is no showman although on this occasion he obviously enjoyed the staging of this private drama.

Finally, in a clearing by the water's edge, we came upon a cupola of branches hiding compounds of tall, stout logs. In one were a dozen sable antelope. A sheep and its lamb bleated incessantly in another, against which had been set a large cage made from steel girders, piping, and stout wire. A wooden platform on the floor of the cage near the live bait operated a trip lever to release a trap door at the other end.

On the island on which we stood were five lions, two male and three female, and three leopards which, with the mainland too far away for them to swim for it, had to be saved by trapping. A lioness had already been caught in the cage three days previously and taken to safety. That night we slept under a stretch of green canvas on a neighbouring island, and returned to the cage before the sun had risen. The trap door was down, and there was a commotion among the animals safe in their stockades. A 3-year-old lioness paced the cage, snarling and clawing at the bars.

"You beauty," murmured Rupert. "What a girl; and only four more to go." A tarpaulin was flung over the cage and the snarling ceased. The cage was rolled on logs to the shore of the island.

Later in the morning we returned in *The Ark* towing a Kon-Tiki style raft of tree trunks and oil drums. Scores of trembling Africans manhandled the cage on to the raft. The tow-lines tightened and dripped pearls in the sunlight as *The Ark* nosed her way out to open water between the blackened fingers of the tops of drowned trees. Rupert squatted by the cage in which the lioness lurched and growled. Guests on the terrace of the Kariba Hotel were being served their lunch-time iced beers and pink gins by white-coated African waiters as the trap door was hauled up and the lioness bounded out to freedom in a Kariba game reserve ringed by smoky-purple, craggy peaks.

Chapter 17

GAME RANCHING

Two American scientists, Dr. Raymond F. Dasmann and Dr. Archie S. Mossman, both Fulbright scholars, shocked ranchers and farmers in Africa in mid-1961 when, after more than a year's research on the *lowveld* of Southern Rhodesia near the South African border, they claimed that breeding wild animals there for meat was not only practical but considerably more profitable than raising cattle.

The two zoologists had been asked to investigate the possibilities of harvesting game as a source of meat for Africans, without jeopardizing its breeding stocks—to try to find a solution, as one conservationist put it, to "the essential problem of helping a meat-eating people to obtain the meat they need without ruining capital stocks of animals or the land on which they live".

Unimproved *lowveld* country barely supports enough cattle to make ranching worth while, but will, however, carry abundant herds of game living in their traditional habitat. Generally, cattle can be supported only after a lengthy and expensive *veld* improvement programme. Even when cattle graze on such open, unforested or thinly-forested grass country which has been improved to the maximum, it is still, in some cases, less profitable than game. Giraffe and zebra, which remain plump and sleek even in drought, are both capable of producing large quantities of meat, even in dry areas where domestic animals would not be likely to survive or certainly to thrive.

"Throughout the world there is a conflict of interest between those who wish to preserve land with its natural life forms for aesthetic or scientific reasons, and those who wish to use it for the production of the immediate necessities of life," declare Drs. Dasmann and Mossman. "This conflict is clearly marked in Africa. Unless it can be resolved in a manner satisfactory to both sides, the rich and varied fauna of the continent have small chance for survival.

"The realization of this has brought a renewed interest in research on African fauna. Much emphasis has been placed on the necessity for establishing the economic value of African wild life. If it can be shown that the wild animals of Africa have sufficient commercial value to enable them to compete economically with domestic livestock, then those who are concerned chiefly with making land produce food or other products to meet immediate needs can be expected to take a greater interest in the preservation and mangement of the wild fauna."

As they state, these considerations were of importance to Drs. Dasmann and Mossman when they arrived in Southern Rhodesia at the end of 1959 to begin their wild life studies, and "we therefore decided on a study which would demonstrate quickly the economic potential of big game mammals."

This was, indeed, a "most urgent" problem in the Colony where over large areas of the country game had disappeared or become very scarce and where one today can drive for hundreds of road-miles without seeing even a rock-rabbit.

"Throughout the Native reserves and the European farmlands game was being eliminated at an accelerating rate. Aesthetic and scientific arguments had little effect on those who wanted to produce domestic livestock on lands occupied by game. Protective game laws stood for little. Only economic arguments seemed likely to appeal to the pastoralist."

The work of Drs. Dasmann and Mossman was concentrated on a ranch of 135,000 acres belonging to Henderson and Sons (Pvt.) Ltd., 130 miles south-east of Southern Rhodesia's second city, Bulawayo.

"Although European ranches do not present as desperate a problem as the Native reserves, we believed that a management programme could be more quickly carried out on private land and its results could then apply to Native reserves and national land," the two men reported in a paper presented to a meeting of the National Affairs Association in Bulawayo in March, 1961. "The Hendersons had a long standing interest in wild game and had endeavoured to protect it. But, caught in the conflict between the economics of ranching and a desire to conserve game, they had decided to develop the ranch for livestock. This brought the need for fencing, water development and construction of other facilities for cattle. These, in turn, brought conflicts with game. When we arrived, approximately half the ranch had been developed to some extent for cattle, with the rest supporting only game."

A fifty-square-mile area of the ranch, stretching from the Umzingwane River eastwards fifteen miles to the main road to Bulawayo, served as the zoologists' principal study area.

The findings, however, are generally applicable to a surrounding area of an additional sixty-five square-miles. The remaining ninety square-miles of the ranch are stocked with cattle along with game, but otherwise do not differ greatly from the cattle-free study area.

The country at Hendersons', like most of the southern *lowveld* of Rhodesia, is flat, but broken at intervals by granite *kopjes* which range in height from tree level up to several hundred feet. It is dissected by numerous steep-banked stream courses which drain into the Umzingwane River, but only carry a flow of water during wet weather; at other times this is found on the surface in a few scattered pools. The rainfall is normally between twelve inches and twenty inches annually, but is highly variable. Their year of study was a drought year, with a poorly-distributed rainfall which totalled about eight inches.

After describing the relatively uniform vegetation on the ranch, with *mopani* the most characteristic and widespread tree, Drs. Dasmann and Mossman add: "Game is distributed throughout the ranch, but its abundance locally varies with the season. The spatial relationship of food and cover to surface water governs the distribution and abundance of animals. During the wet season most species are widely scattered. In the dry season most concentrate in a strip within a few miles of the river.

"In order to determine the economic value of game in an area, it is necessary to determine the numbers of animals present of each species; to find out the extent to which they are resident on the area through the year; and to discover the rate at which young are produced and survive. From this one can discover how large an annual crop may safely be removed from the game populations. If provisions are then made for obtaining and marketing this annual crop, the value of the game can be determined and comparisons made with the annual income that would be obtained if the land were used, instead, for some other purpose.

"One of our first tasks on starting work was to determine the numbers and distribution of animals on the ranch throughout the various seasons. With the time and facilities available, it was obviously impossible to determine exact numbers of animals. We sought instead to determine a safe minimum population figure which would serve as a base from which to start a cropping programme. We attempted also to determine whether or not this population remained on the ranch during both wet and dry seasons."

To do this they made principal use of road strip-counts, with supplementary information provided by area-counts from *kopjes*, spoor-counts and general observations.

"In addition to obtaining a minimum population figure and information on distribution of game, we also sought to determine the productivity and potential yield from the game populations. This was done through regular sex and age classification counts, observations of behaviour and the collection of specimens for biological examination . . . by these techniques we were able to obtain the information essential to start on a commercial game-cropping programme.

"As we were carrying out game studies on the ranch, plans for developing the ranch for cattle were going inexorably forward. It soon became obvious that unless we could demonstrate quickly not only the potential economic value of game, but the practicability of the marketing of it, there would soon be no area left for the wild animals. Our work would then have only some theoretical value, to be argued about in the future as game populations elsewhere continued to disappear."

By the start of the 1960 dry season, they believed that they knew enough about the game on the ranch to start a trial game-cropping programme. They knew that the ranch supported a large, resident game population which produced considerable numbers of young and they felt they could make a safe estimate about the potential sustained yield. In May, 1960, they recommended a game-cropping programme to the ranch owners, who agreed to try it out. A proposal was submitted to the Department of Wild Life Conservation, recommending a harvest of over 1,100 game mammals, the bulk being impala and zebra, and a permit was issued authorizing the ranch owners to take these animals.

"It was next necessary to arrange for the marketing of fresh meat and biltong, and to obtain permits for this. It was near the end of July before arrangements would permit the opening shots of the game harvest, and August before the first truck-load of venison was on its way to the butchers. This was unfortunate in that we missed several months of dry, cold weather and began the harvest at a time when the days were getting warm.

"We undertook game-cropping with considerable trepidation. We were concerned that shooting might make some species so wary that it would be impossible to obtain a good harvest, and might make other species move out of the area. Consequently, we decided against using traditional sport-hunting methods which create disturbance and looked to poachers and market hunters for our techniques. Because this was to be an experimental commercial operation, carried out in the interest of long-term game conservation, techniques which were both efficient and inexpensive, however unorthodox, were authorized by the Director of Wild Life Conservation.

"We ruled out day-time hunting under conditions where the hunter would be seen or his scent detected by the animals being hunted. Every effort was made to dissociate the sight and scent of man and vehicles from the noise and disturbance of shooting. Consequently, the two chief hunting methods that were used were day-time shooting from blinds, and night hunting with a spotlight.

"Blinds were constructed at waterholes, downwind from where the game would drink. These were entered only when no game was present, and once established the hunter was not permitted to leave the blind while game was in the vicinity. Night hunting was done from a Land-Rover, using a powerful spotlight. In addition to hunting, we experimented with the deadly weapon of the African poacher, the snare. Snares, as employed by most poachers, are both inhumane and inefficient. Through some experimenting, however, it was possible to devise a type of snare that was effective and reasonably humane . . . with the two hunting techniques it was possible to obtain all of the game that we required for trial marketing. The remaining animals were not disturbed when these methods were used. Following a heavy day's shooting at a water-hole, we could return on the following day in a vehicle or on foot and have large numbers of animals stand to stare at us, not associating the previous day's disturbance with man at all."

Game meat was then marketed through butcheries in Bulawayo at the following prices:

Duiker, Steenbuck:	1s. 6d. per lb.
Impala:	1s. 3d. per lb.
Wildebeest, Kudu, Warthog:	1s. 0d. per lb.
Buffalo:	10d. per lb.
Game biltong, first grade:	4s. 6d. per lb.
Game biltong, second grade:	1s. 0d. per lb.

At these prices an adult animal of the various game species on the ranch had the following value for meat alone:

Impala:	65 lb.	£4
Zebra:	Biltong	£8
Kudu:	225 lb.	£11
Wildebeest:	260 lb.	£13
Buffalo:	570 lb.	£24
Duiker:	20 lb.	£1 10s.
Steenbuck:	12 lb.	18s. 0d.
Warthog:	70 lb.	£3 10s.

During the period of game-cropping and marketing in 1960, over 450 head of game, mostly impala and zebra, were shot and either trucked to market in Bulawayo, or used on the ranch for African rations.

"In addition, losses, particularly in the early stages of the programme, brought the total kill to about 500 animals. Besides these, at least 150 head were reported as killed earlier in the year in sport-shooting, scientific collecting or for ranch rations. The total kill was probably much larger than this, for all was not reported. It is probable, therefore, that at least 750 head of game, mostly impala and zebra, were removed through legal shooting during 1960. Additional animals were killed by poachers.

"Predators, including lions, leopards, wild dogs and smaller carnivores, took a considerable toll. Accidents of various kinds brought considerable mortality. Towards the end of the dry season there was much mortality among the zebra in particular, and also among other grazing species, probably caused by inadequate nutrition.

"Despite all of this, the game populations were as large or larger at the end of 1960 as they were at the start of our studies. The response of the game populations to the 1960 kill, in addition to the more complete and realistic figures we have been able to obtain on total numbers, permitted us to recommend a game harvest for 1961 that is well above that recommended for 1960."

From the work done during the cropping and marketing period, it was possible for Drs. Dasmann and Mossman to evaluate the economics of game ranching at Henderson's, assuming that adequate markets could be found.

"We have been most concerned with the question of how game compares with cattle in producing an income. Part of the ranch is at present supporting cattle, and in making our calculations we assume that it will continue to do so. However, the important issue is whether or not the remainder of the ranch should be developed for cattle at the expense of game.

"To compare game with cattle, it is best to consider only the fifty-square-mile area for which our figures are more reliable. This, if *kopjes* and other waste areas are excluded, is about 30,000 acres suited to cattle ranching. The economics of developing and operating a 30,000-acre cattle ranch in the southern *lowveld* of Rhodesia have been studied in detail by the Hendersons in association with H. H. Fraser (Rhod.) (Pvt.) Ltd. and published in a private report. These figures will be used. Such an area, stocked at one beast per thirty acres, would support 1,000 animal units, or

1,155 head of cattle, if developed. In this region a 60 per cent calving rate can be expected, and an annual mortality of 2·9 per cent. This herd would therefore produce an annual crop of 189 head of cattle, marketed at close to four years of age. These could be sold for £5,198 as a gross income.

"However, the costs of development, maintenance and operation of a ranch of this size for cattle would amount to £4,692 per year, which would leave a net annual income of only £506. If the area could be improved and stocked at a rate of twenty acres per animal unit, it could yield 284 marketable beasts per year, for an income of £7,797 gross, or £2,500 net profit. This, however, would require some years of *veld* improvement work, which would necessarily be added to the costs of development of the ranch.

"By contrast the same area, under present conditions and without development, could yield a gross annual income of £5,500 from game. From this would have to be deducted the costs of production, which include the salary of a game manager and his assistants, transportation, tools and materials, etc. A net profit of somewhat over £3,200 per year would be left. Wastage and accidents of various kinds could reduce this, but it would nevertheless well exceed the net income that could be expected from cattle, even at a stocking rate of twenty acres per cow.

"Another important consideration is whether the area will produce more beef or venison per acre. Here an adequate comparison is more difficult to make. The land is presently supporting game. Under present conditions it could support few cattle, because there is little grass near the river, where water is found, and no water in the dry season where the grass is to be found.

"However, if it were developed for cattle, with fencing, water development, etc., it could at a stocking rate of thirty acres per cow, yield 94,500 lb. of meat per year. This is a yield of 3 lb. of beef, or 6 lb. of animal weight, per acre per year. Our recommended game crop for 1961 would amount to 118,300 lb. of marketable meat (dressed carcasses) or approximately 4 lb. of venison per acre. We do not know how much more game meat it would yield if it were developed for game to the extent we are assuming it would be developed for cattle."

The two scientists stated that, although their population estimates were conservative, it might prove that the cropping rate for some species was too high.

"However, it is equally likely that for other species the rates can be increased. Only trial will provide the answer, but at this stage we believe that the critical question is not whether or not the game will stand this rate of cropping, but whether or not adequate markets for the meat can be found.

"*From the work that has been done in Southern Rhodesia thus far, there seems little reason to doubt that game ranching is both practical and economically feasible. Assuming that markets can be developed and that the prices received by the rancher are maintained at the present levels, game can yield a greater net profit to the land owner than cattle on lands that require twenty to thirty acres or more to support a cow, in regions similar to those in which we have worked. On lands with a carrying capacity of one cow per thirty acres, game can yield more meat, without any capital being spent on development, than cattle can yield after the land has been developed.*

"On some lands, cattle ranch development may result in higher meat yields than can be had with no development for game. How much these lands would yield from game, with some development to improve the game habitat, remains to be determined."

They stress there is much to be learned about game ranching, particularly about the ecology of game populations. Much of this information, they state, can only be learned through continued game ranching. Regardless of how much was known about the biology of a species, its reaction, as a population, to heavy shooting had to be determined by shooting. The estimates presented had been conservative. In calculating the value of game products, they had included only the value of the dressed carcass and had ignored the considerable value of the hides and other by-products.

They had also considered only the ungulates and had ignored the meat yield and market value from small mammals, ostrich and game birds. All of these values were high. Also ignored was the income to be obtained through marketing hides of various carnivores, many of which had high value.

The potential income to be derived by charging for the privilege of hunting trophy animals such as lion, buffalo, leopard, kudu and others had also not been included. The authors of the paper emphasize that they had been working in an area that was not outstanding for either game numbers or variety. At least two species, elephant and sable, were no longer resident on the ranch, and, from all accounts, wildebeest existed there in much smaller numbers than formerly. Many other places in Rhodesia supported more game. It could reasonably be expected that some attention to game management and the ecological requirements of the various species would yield dividends in terms of an increased yield of game products from Henderson's ranch.

The verdict of Drs. Dasmann and Mossman is that the success or failure of game ranching in Southern Rhodesia depends less on whether the details of numbers, production and yield for game populations can be worked out than on the part the Government will play in developing markets and facilitating the marketing of game meat, hides and by-products.

"The marketing problem is critical," they declared. "The meat can be produced; the demand for the meat is present among the African population of Rhodesia; what remains is to provide the proper channels from producer to consumer. This is a job for the Government. Unless the Government plays an active part now, the existing and contemplated game ranching programmes will be abandoned. Once abandoned, it will be most difficult to start them again.

"It is our hope that the work reported here will give an impetus to the movement towards sustained yield management of African game for commercial purposes. It is our belief that only this economic approach can save game from extermination over broad areas of Africa. It is also our belief that the time to start management of game on an economic basis is now. Delays, whether in the interests of additional research, or through sheer governmental inertia, can only increase the chances of failure."

Chapter 18

TAME ELAND

FOLLOWING the lead given by the zoologists and with the blessing of the Government, several cattle ranchers in the southern part of Southern Rhodesia boldly began the experiment of profitable game harvesting, giving European and African families new, cheaper-than-beef meat dishes and cutting house-wives' shopping bills.

A large meat-canning concern in the West Nicholson area tested the canning of impala taken from their own and the Henderson ranches. I was given a labelled tin of "Game Pate" and one of "Game Steak in Wine". Both tasted excellent, but a representative of the company said that, because of the public attitude to canned meats in general, there would be no hasty decisions regarding the commercial sale of tinned game products at home or abroad. Markets for game ranchers remained mainly confined to butchers' shops in their areas, selling mostly to Africans, when larger markets provided by the Government or major private enterprises, or both, were sorely needed.

The Southern Rhodesia Government has agreed in principle to establish an experimental game farm on the *lowveld* on which the ranching of antelope for meat production as an economic proposi-tion will be investigated. Mr. J. H. R. Savory, Director of Irriga-tion and Secretary for Lands, stated in a report tabled in Parliament that preliminary investigations had indicated "good prospects" for the development of this type of farming. The report pointed out that in various countries in Eastern and Southern Africa eland

in particular had been tamed and herds built. It was still necessary
to test whether this animal could be ranched on a large scale and
economically. It was possible, the report added, that other species
might also justify experiments on these lines.

First experiments involve the farming mainly of larger
antelope such as eland and impala. Game farming on a farm, as
distinct from a ranch, entails the domestication of wild animals
and, therefore, only a few species are suitable. Eland can become
more docile in captivity than cattle, and often graze with cattle.
They can, however, leap conventional cattle fencing and farmers
have been warned that it might be necessary to erect higher
fences.

Eland have been marketed for body meat alone by Mr. John
Posselt of Southern Rhodesia's Department of Native Affairs at
£30 for a 3½-year-old ox.

It is an over-simplification to say baldly that game are markedly
more resistant to endemic diseases than domestic cattle, but one
scientist in Bulawayo who had been concerned with the segrega-
tion, raising and culling of middle-bracket wild beasts for meat-
marketing put it this way: "Over a million years the game
animals of Africa have become resistant to *some* of the parasites of
endemic diseases. They have learnt to live with them."

Whereas in some areas domestic cattle may require both dipping
and inoculation to combat disease, so far as game is concerned
this is necessary only in those cases where the wild animals have
(as eland can) become domesticated to the point where they run
with the cattle in what is, after all, simply a new form of mixed
farming.

As stated elsewhere, a notable example of this is the virtual
immunity of wild animals in Africa to the trypanosomes transferred to them by the tsetse fly. Malignant catarrh, which is not
generally fatal, affects only cattle and not the wildebeest which
carry it. Yet a number of animal diseases are inter-communicable
between domestic stock and game, and some wild animals are
liable to contract the same diseases, such as foot and mouth, as

cattle. Some sixty years ago, an epidemic of the malignant and contagious rinderpest wiped out both cattle and game herds in Africa. Veterinary surgeons claim that, generally speaking, most of the serious cattle diseases such as rinderpest are carried by various species of antelope which, however, now appear to be immune from it.

The conservationists reply that vets are inclined to insist that because a particular disease is recorded in a wild animal it is carried by the species. Both sides agree that a monumental amount of research into the carrying and transfer of diseases by both domesticated and wild animals still remains to be undertaken, and that the whole subject is a very long way from being thoroughly understood.

Game harvesting on a controlled, ranching basis, like a sea or lake fishing industry, must not be compared with cattle farming. If a disease breaks out, the fish are not netted; as a parallel, game killings would be suspended until the epidemic had abated.

The belief that game farming may well result in a new form of land usage of considerable importance to the economy of Southern Rhodesia has been propounded by Mr. Thane Riney, an American Fulbright scholar who has made a two-year study of game husbandry in the Colony.

The Department of Wild Life Conservation in Southern Rhodesia is propagating the view that if more farmers went in for game raising it would greatly help the preservation of wild animals in the country. The farmers would not only keep the game in a healthy state, but would also contribute to the nation-wide campaign of putting down poaching.

Rescues of zebra, impala, buffalo, kudu, sable antelope, bush-buck and other animals from doomed islands on Lake Kariba have given Mr. Eric Noble, a veteran hunter and wild life conservationist, enough stock to start an approved pilot game farm on forty acres at Umtali in the Colony's rugged and mountainous eastern districts.

At the end of October, 1961, I visited the Henderson ranchland where for that year Drs. Dasmann and Mossman had recommended a crop of about 2,600 head of game which would yield more than 300,000 lb. of dressed carcasses with a market value of some £15,000, leaving a net profit of £8,400. Markets in Britain, France and Germany were being explored, and frozen impala meat from the ranch was already being sold in butchers' shops in Holland.

To popularize venison and boost sales by attracting white customers, 28-year-old, Rhodesian-born Peter Johnstone, a serious-minded former tsetse control officer, now Game Manager on the ranch and something of a *veld* gourmet, had compiled a number of recipes to be printed and distributed among butchers in Bulawayo. Barbecued spare-ribs of impala or duiker should be eaten, he recommends, with a sauce made of cider vinegar, sugar, Worcester sauce, tomato sauce, salt, mustard, paprika, pepper and garlic, while venison steaks and chops could be sprinkled with garlic salt and carraway seeds while frying.

"Warthogs are ugly looking fellows," says Peter, "but their flesh is delicious. It tastes like pork."

Here is the recipe for his own "Gamekeeper's Pie":

Take 1½ lb. of minced venison and one chopped onion. Put in a pan, cover with water, and cook until well done and thickened. In the meantime, boil several potatoes and mash them. To the cooked meat add one tablespoon of tomato sauce; salt and pepper to taste. Thicken further with a little gravy powder or flour and pour into an oven-proof dish. Cover with the mashed potatoes and bake until browned on top.

On the grass outside Peter's cottage were hundreds of skulls of zebra which he had shot on the ranch under the controlled cropping programme. Each skull was tagged with the sex and weight of the animal whose age structure is determined, like a horse, from the teeth. There were zebra, kudu, waterbuck and giraffe skeletons in a tree above the skulls.

We strolled across to the ranch butchery where Africans were cutting up shot zebra mares. Pushing his faded pork-pie hat back on his head, Peter told me that the zebra meat was cut into strips, dried in the sun on racks near the butchery, and sold as biltong which looks like plugged tobacco. The Boers fought the British on biltong in the South African War, but today, cut into wafers, it is served as a tasty snack at most cocktail parties in southern Africa.

Impala, kudu, wildebeest, duiker and steenbuck skins had been laid out, awaiting the merchants. Long strips of buffalo hide, used mainly in neighbouring South Africa by Afrikaans farmers for haltering oxen, were being stretched and cured from the limbs of a tree in which hung the foot of a rogue elephant shot while tramping down cattle fences some years before.

Game, according to Peter Johnstone, dressed out much more economically than cattle at an average of 63 per cent for kudu, 61 per cent for impala, 65 per cent for young giraffe and 53 per cent for buffalo which are the only animals rivalling cattle in damaging the *veld*. He said that second-grade game biltong had risen from 1s. to 1s. 6d. per pound, and even game livers were fetching 1s. 6d. a pound.

"You can buy land around here for 3s. 6d. an acre, and the first thing the purchaser does is to kill off all the game to make way for cattle," said Peter. "Most of the game in Southern Rhodesia is being lost through people wiping out the wild animals on their ranches. Game ranching could save them for it is true to say that no rancher or farmer will preserve game merely for the sake of preservation. Administrators insist that human rights come first—human rights seem to mean freedom for humans to destroy the wild-life habitat."

He feels game will be saved only if its economic value is realized and used for hunting sport, its aesthetic value, and protein production on its own, and with cattle. Hundreds of head of game, principally zebra and wildebeest, were exterminated on ranches for the "sin" of breaking fences occasionally (their sale value more than paid for repairs) and the fact that they eat grass. No one knew if they used grass more efficiently than cattle, but they easily walked much farther to water than cattle.

After elephants, zebra were the best diggers for water in river sand, a fact not widely known. They were often the saviours in drought of many animals and birds.

"Fences, continuous disturbances by herd-boys, Africans, dogs and shooting are weeding down game herds rapidly. The African plain-wire snarer is the worst of the lot. If a poacher here catches a zebra in a snare and does not want to eat it, he cuts the wire if it is still alive and allows it to go off for fear it will die near his snares and attract vultures and, consequently, some form of authority to catch him and give him a prison sentence.

"Another thing that is killing off game is the Government's lack of foresight in allowing areas to become grossly overstocked with game, causing losses from starvation and, worse still, irreparable damage to the *veld*. In this country, as in many others in Africa, the game laws are good, but may not, in fact, exist for all the good they do at times."

I did not have the opportunity of going out night hunting with Peter, but he outlined the method. Impala are caught in the beam of a spotlight of his Land-Rover; if they attempt to escape they are herded by a wire-haired terrier which he uses as a hunting dog. Both to avoid the noise of shots setting to flight other animals in the vicinity and to preserve the hide, the throat of the animal is swiftly and expertly cut with a razor-sharp knife.

A clotted-cream-coloured hunter's moon was growing pale when I set out with Peter at five o'clock in the morning to tour the ranch. His chief African tracker stopped a herd of running buffalo by imitating the faltering bellows of a calf in distress. A master of this art, he uses similar distress calls to halt zebra and wildebeest for counting or shooting.

We inspected Peter's lines of snares set in the thorn bushes. For zebra and wildebeest he uses a 15-ft. long quarter-inch cable soft wire rope with a Crosby clamp set 25 in. from the eye of the noose so that the trapped animals are not throttled. Thinner snares, on the same principles, are used for impala. Peter said that 95 per cent of all animals caught were found alive and uninjured in the snares. They are shot or their throats are cut.

A herd of zebra scampered off through the trees. "We'll have one of those," exclaimed Peter, stopping the Land-Rover and reaching for his rifle. (He carries an elephant's eyelid hair as a spare sight for the gun, for luck.)

Peter disappeared with his trackers, and minutes later two shots were heard in quick succession. Guided by patches of trampled grass and blood spots on the leaves of bushes, the chief tracker led me to a spot three quarters of a mile from the road where lay the body of a 740-lb. zebra stallion. The first shot had broken a hind leg; the second, fired into the rectum to avoid damage to the skin, had killed the animal instantaneously. The Africans had cut open the stomach and were removing the entrails before turning the body over to drain. They covered it with leaves and grass to keep off the vultures.

"Zebra tolerate shooting hunting better than any other wild animal," Peter told me when he returned with the Land-Rover. "I have often been called a bloodthirsty bastard by people who don't understand my job."

The zebra was loaded into the vehicle; one African pulled on the tail and his companions hauled on buffalo-hide ropes round the carcass, to be taken the five miles to the butchery.

On the journey we stopped to watch giraffe, as graceful as on the plains, weaving between the concentrations of *mopani* at a gallop without colliding with a single tree. Sighting another group of zeba, Peter took aim and fired. A miss? We went half a mile into the trees before looking for blood patches and other signs before deciding the animal had not been hit. There were distinctive sounds, said Peter, by which it could be told where a zebra had been hit. A shot in the stomach with a hard-nosed bullet sounded like "go-toop", in the shoulder "klup-zing" and in the hind quarters "kuh-eh".

At noon we drove to a straw and sacking blind by a small dam and, conversing in whispers, waited for the animals to come in to drink. Twenty ostrich chicks, which Peter calculated were no more than four days old, were the first to arrive, followed by the parent birds. When they had gone, an impala appeared at the water's edge. It died at a single cough from Peter's rifle which had a silencer.

Passing the snare-line later in the day we saw a 100-lb. impala ram struggling and kicking in a noose. Grappling with the frightened animal, Peter gently freed the ram—"We don't need this one for the market"—which bounded away unhurt.

Chapter 19

SNAKES AND LADDERS

THIRTY thousand copies of the old game of Snakes and Ladders with a new African background have been distributed free to African children in Southern Rhodesia by the enterprising and far-sighted Natural Resources Board.

"In this particular game you go up ladders for conserving the country's wild life and down the snakes for a variety of sins, varying from starting grass fires to poisoning fish," said a spokesman of the Board. "The idea is to instil in the minds of African children certain of the good and bad conservation practices."

The scheme captured the interest of international conservation experts, and copies of the game were sent for distribution in other African countries. Laudably, Southern Rhodesia has taken to heart the exhortations of experts to build game conservation into the educational system, and the authorities' "get 'em young" policy has paid off and set an example to other lands. Apart from the Natural Resources Board, the full weight of the Federal Tourist Board, the National Parks Department and wild life associations was behind the energetic "Conserve, don't destroy" campaign.

Schools responded "magnificently" to painting, drawing and modelling competitions. In the Bulawayo area, fourteen schools earned certificates of merit. Photographers, both professional and amateur, played their part with exhibitions and by entering organized competitions. Hundreds of children entered for a colouring-in competition which had as its propaganda effect an appreciation of wild animals. Four thousand people took part in radio quizzes. Special wild life articles which appeared in African newspapers resulted in demands for 40,000 copies of the articles. Some 3,000 coloured wall charts of animals for identification were produced; 3,000 sets of miniature animals were made and 3,000 card albums were distributed free.

The prize-winning poster in a nation-wide competition—it showed a hunter with half-gun and half-camera above the slogan "Don't destroy, let's enjoy"—aroused the admiration of a prominent German naturalist who wrote to the Board saying it was the finest poster of its kind he had ever seen, and asked for permission to use a reproduction in a German magazine.

"Every possible medium to get through to the masses was used," the Board reported. "Competitions, lectures, film shows and advertising, with the aid and co-operation of commercial enterprises, were among the main media of putting across the theme of conservation."

Expressing gratification at the success of the campaign, the report added: "But this does not mean there is room for complacency. The fight to impress on people of all ages and colours the immense value of our heritage has to go on."

It was announced in March, 1962, that at least fifty post-graduate students were expected to enrol for a one-year wild life conservation course being offered by the multi-racial University College of Rhodesia and Nyasaland in Salisbury. Most of the students for the course, scheduled to start in 1963 and first of its kind in Africa, are expected to come from government departments. The course, said to have created "a tremendous amount of interest", will cover all aspects of wild-life conservation, and instruction will be centred on the zoology department of the College.

A mammoth census of the wild-life population of Southern Rhodesia is being undertaken by the Department of Wild Life Conservation in conjunction with the National Museum, and people throughout the country who are in a position to observe game in their areas are helping. Questionnaires were sent to farmers, ranchers, foresters, land development officers, wild-life conservation officers and wardens asking them to give details of game in their districts, to indicate if they have noticed an increase or decrease in the number of wild animals, and to record the movements and habits of game.

The Department of Wild Life Conservation, the Veterinary Services and the Natural Resources Board combines, in the first quarter of 1962 to launch a national appeal for funds to re-introduce white rhino to the country. In their writings the pioneer hunter Selous and others established the fact that the white rhino were present in the Gwaai Valley and elsewhere in the Colony in the early days but owing to uncontrolled shooting, became extinct round about the turn of the century. The Federal and Southern Rhodesian Governments have each donated £1,000 towards the estimated total cost of transporting eight white rhino in crates by road 1,000 miles from Natal, cost of capture and transport being about £500 an animal. Two pairs went to the Matopos National Park and two other pairs to a beautiful new game sanctuary in the Kyle Dam area.

*   *   *

As with Kenya's Masai leaders and Africans in Tanganyika, there is a new spirit abroad among the African authorities in self-governing Uganda towards wild animals. There are marked and encouraging signs that they realize that wild life is an economic legacy which must be developed and controlled like any other national bounty if full benefit is to be obtained from it. It is not so many years ago since the Bunyoro Kingdom Parliament, reflecting the general attitude of African local governments, passed a resolution deploring the fact that the country was being turned into a zoo, and added a rider that the function of the game department should be to protect people from wild animals—"but instead it seems to be protecting the wild animals from people."

The attitude of the African local governments has, gratifyingly, changed radically and today several of them are asking for parks, reserves and controlled-hunting areas to be established in their territories. After the Karamoja District Council passed a resolution by twenty-one votes to three asking for the Kidepo Valley in the north to be declared a national park, the resolution came before the Legislative Council for ratification. Some Opposition members criticized it. But no one voted against it.

In addition to being a new tourist attraction, the Kidepo Park will provide a reservoir of game for the controlled-hunting areas which the Uganda Wild Life Company has developed round its borders. This dual-purpose role is part of Uganda's dynamic new game policy which has aroused the keen interest, and self-interest, of the Africans in control of the country and their followers.

During the International Conference on Wild Life at Arusha conference, African speakers appealed for a greater understanding by their people of the value of wild life and, in a paper explaining that tourism could substantially help to raise the African standard of living, the Tanganyika Minister responsible for game conservation emphasized that Africans must be convinced that animals in their parks and reserves were more use to them alive than dead and that money was as well spent in preserving the animals as on schools.

* * *

After coffee, tourism provides the second largest source of Kenya's income. The total revenue from tourism in the territories of East Africa is now said to be between £8,000,000 and £10,000,000 a year, and, with appropriate publicity and improved and extended accommodation, the number of visitors, and accordingly, the revenue, could well be doubled or trebled. The revenue derived from tourists to East Africa comes mainly from their expenditures on hotels, equipment, *safari* transport, game licences, souvenirs, photography, mounting of trophies and entrance, accommodation and other fees in national parks.

Tourism, measured there annually in several millions of pounds, has been acknowledged as potentially Kenya's greatest money earner, but so much depends on the existence and availability of game animals. The number of visitors to the Colony has been falling off, and if the word gets around, as some tourists agents say it already has, that rhino and lion and elephant are difficult to find, it is feared there may be a further slump.

It has been worked out that the average visitor, and he comes to see the animals, spends twenty-days in East Africa, fourteen of them in Kenya, and spends an average of £6 each day. The East African Tourist Travel Association, which represents government airlines, hotels and commercial firms, pressed for tax concessions to encourage capital investment in tourism, for the reduction of Customs and immigration formalities and for a wide extension and improvement of tourist facilities.

On a "top-bracket" hunting or photographic *safari* in Kenya it costs a single person an average of £40 a day, a sum which would keep an African servant in food for nearly a year.

There are instances, certainly, of degrees of exploitation of tourists in East Africa, whether by shady or mushroom firms or crusading officials determined to wring every shilling out of the visitor to help sustain the parks.

There are *safari* firms in Kenya which argue that high charges serve to attract rich Americans and other wealthy amateur big-game hunters, who are provided with every possible comfort and safety measure from the time they are picked up at the airport at Nairobi until being returned to it, perhaps with the skin of a lion which, in all probability and unknown to him, has been shot simultaneously over the visitor's shoulder by the professional hunter who, under the Colony's laws, is obliged to accompany the client.

"A lot of people come here and want their money back if they can't shoot at least two animals a day," a white hunter in Nairobi told me. "But anybody can hunt in Tanganyika or Rhodesia alone, hire a Land-Rover and have all the thrills and trophies he wants. We supply the padding. That's how we live." He suggested the capture and sale of big game alive—as much as £700, he said, could be obtained for a young elephant—to help to save all the game.

Men in the Kenya hunting *safari* business are worried what will happen with the coming of independence and whether the African leaders, at the behest of their black electorates, might curb or end this "Muzungu" (European) sport. "The Africans' indiscriminate killing of game is quite different from the bag of the strictly-controlled tourist hunter," say the white hunters. "The former can do only harm to the country, the latter can bring only good. Large-scale slaughter of animals means that eventually all the game disappears. When the game goes, there are no more hunting *safaris* and no more cash."

*   *   *

Uganda's parks—visited by about 5,000 people every year—and reserves are no longer to be kept like natural zoos. Even within the parks, game management to produce the optium population and distribution of animals will include regular cropping of the natural increase. This is a long-overdue system which must be followed in other African parks.

Outside the parks, the Uganda Wild Life Company is establishing *safari* lodges from which game-watching and hunting can be done, by the "little man" at cut prices the hunting being under controlled conditions which will ensure that all species in the area continue to flourish. And, most important of all, the meat from the cropping and profits from tourism and hunting are being handed over to the African people in whose territory the game-lands lie. This helps tribal authorities to realize that, controlled and developed as a continuing asset, their game lands will yield them much higher rewards than they can get from indiscriminate extermination of game or its replacement with herds of cattle.

The Kenya Wild Life Society, stressing the commercial outlook, states that a growing number of package tours will have to be developed out of all proportion to the existing scope if the true commercial value of wild life is to be proved to the people of Africa, and if the essential idea of preservation is to be "sold" to them.

"Only if it is proved beyond shadow of doubt that schools, piped-water supplies, dispensaries and similar ingredients of better living can be attained by means of wild life, exploited by large-scale tourism, will the idea really be sold, accepted and eagerly supported.

"It is no good holding up our hands in horror and saying that package tourists in thousands imply empty bottles, crumpled cartons and waste paper littering the precincts of beauty spots and spoiling the freshness and sense of privacy that has had so much appeal to the comparatively few who have known them in the past. Of course they will, but this is the price that has got to be paid for two inestimable benefits.

"Firstly, an appreciable proportion of the tourists themselves will become ardent supporters of wild-life preservation, and it must never be forgotten that in the modern world it is numbers that count; secondly, wild life will have to be preserved in places to which tourists will never penetrate so that these areas can act as reservoirs for the places where the tourists will always congregate.

"It is a fortunate fact that wild life only resents the presence of Man when Man is recognizable as another animal. When man is disguised by association with a machine he ceases to be a disturbing factor. If, therefore, tourists in the mass are generally kept in vehicles and directed to defined routes and places—East Africa is big enough for plenty of them—there should be no serious disruption of animal life in the terrain. Moreover if waterholes and salt licks, which can be classed as among the animals' chief desires, are provided sufficiently close to these routes and places, there will always be plenty of wild life for the tourists to see and to photograph. Equally there will still be places less accessible and less

Zebra can thrive and grow fat in terrain on which domestic cattle can only with difficulty sustain life. Selective shooting with silenced rifles keeps numbers down and provides meat for sale. It does not terrify the animals. The use of wire by poachers, either as a noose or, as *below*, strung as an obstacle designed to break the neck of a terrified animal driven into it, often inflicts suffering. Africans living in the area usually sympathize with the slayers, so generally it is difficult to bring them to justice unless, as in this case, wardens catch them red-handed.

Left : A rope halter is ready.

Below : Ken Randall drives his Jeep into a herd of buffalo, one of the most dangerous animals in Africa. The head boy is refixing the noose after a buffalo had thrown off the rope. Eventually the animal nearest the right front wheel was captured when Randall held on to its tail !

Right: A young eland has just been hauled to a standstill by a rope which was slipped over its head while it was in full flight. The eland is one of the largest and shyest antelopes in Africa but trials have shown that if it is caught young and kept in close confinement for a time it can be herded like cattle.

Above: John Mills, the game warden at Mbarara in Uganda, inspects a corral which has been erected in the bush to hold captured buffalo. The truck which carries the crated animal to the corral is seen on the right.

Above: Ten newly-captured eland calves in a pen near Mbarara in Uganda where they are being "acclimatized" to a life in captivity. Eventually they become used to the sight of man and can be released into paddocks like cattle, even allowed to run free. *Right:* A tame herd of adult eland quite unconcerned by the presence of a tractor.

directly attractive to man, where the deep calm of primeval Africa will still brood over the face of the land, and where the nature of life need not be geared to the pace and change prevailing in the present century.

"We must today face quite clearly and without illusion the facts of modern Africa, and we must recognize equally clearly the ends towards which we are striving and the means whereby we can best attain them. The basis of all success is effort and the fuel that turns effort into productive activity is money."

Such cries everywhere throughout the African gamelands for money have, naturally, a shrill urgency, but in the past much has been recklessly squandered. Thane Riney calculates that in the twenty-five years, from 1933 to 1958, of an anti-tsetse campaign, the wild animal equivalent of 31,000 tons of meat was shot, representing a cash value of the meat alone at over £3,500,000; that takes no account of the value of hides, trophies and bones.

No large outlay of capital is required where it is decided to use a tsetse area for game raising and cropping.

The gregarious lechwe antelope of Northern Rhodesia's Kafue flood plain is a handsome and timid animal which, when alarmed, runs swiftly with its nose down like a hound on the scent. The male of the species has long, tapering horns and, like the female, is a good swimmer. During the annual inundations, the flats grow a rich crop of lush swamp grass and the lechwe come down across the plain to the marsh border to drink and eat the grasses, wading deep in the swamp waters. Their droppings in the water, as in the case of hippo, nourish vegetable growths which are favoured by bream and other fish.

The gentle lechwe, which has a higher potential protein-per-acre value than good cattle, is doomed unless controlled cropping is introduced. In twenty-eight years (from 1934), the lechwe herds of the Kafue Flats have been reduced by 220,000 to a dwindling total of under 30,000 as a result of mass hunts, known as *chilas*, in which African tribesmen and their women and dogs drive thousands of the antelope into the water and spear them to death in a bloody orgy of killing. The pitful lechwe numbers could, it is estimated, be raised to 100,000 or more, allowing for an annual cropping of a 20,000 surplus representing 2,000 tons of meat.

* * *

The Baila buffalo hunt which I have described is viewed with mixed feelings. Some critics say it is cruel. Others urge that it should be allowed to go on as a traditional operation. Some point out that the hunt helps to keep down the large numbers of buffalo in the area and at the same time satisfies the meat needs of the Africans. The latter, however, is not now so acute, as the Baila are acquiring an increasing number of cattle in their change over from a warrior to a pastoral life.

The 300 elephants killed annually in the Luangwa Valley of Northern Rhodesia as a control operation are carefully used. They provide more than half a pound of meat a week for every man, woman and child of the 60,000 African population. This gives the lie to the jingle:

> *"East is East and West is West.*
> *Though this may not seem relevant,*
> *You all know how to milk a cow*
> *But you can't muck about with an elephant."*

*

The Republic of South Africa

After his visit in January, 1962, the author reports that the pride of the Boer in his prowess with firearms and the concern of the farmer for his crops caused such slaughter over the years that the wild animal population was vanishing swiftly when the government took action for its preservation. Today in the national parks and on game farms a vastly different picture is apparent.

Chapter 20

A RAVAGED EDEN

THE serpent of the ox-wagon train swayed over the shimmering South African *veld*. Bearded Boers, lashing on the slavering teams with zebra-hide whips, peered at black patches on the yellow scrubland ahead and fumbled for their muzzle-loaders and powder-horns. Their wives, perspiring in poke bonnets and voluminous dresses, clutched the family Bibles and hungrily contemplated the prospect of thick steaks sizzling over the embers of fires that night within the protective circle of the wagon laager. And there would be hides for bartering with the naked tribesmen, ivory tusks for sale to merchants, soft but durable skins for *veldschoen* (moccasins), and dried meat in plenty for emergency rations on this searing nineteenth-century Great Trek from the Cape to the Transvaal.

The ox-wagons lurched on, in to an animal kingdom where all around could be seen masses of buffalo, waterbuck and eland, dense groups of handsome kudu, sable antelope, giraffe and swaggering ostriches. Families of lion and elephant etched the skyline. Boer horsemen, their eyes glinting with the passion of the hunt, galloped in and scattered the herds. Dust clouds mingled with puffs of grey-black rifle smoke as every animal which swerved into range was shot down in a massacre which went on until the sun was low in the west and their ball ammunition was exhausted.

For fifty years such killings continued. Animals were slain for food and other necessities, for trophies, for tusks or plumes and for lion and leopard skins. Before the discovery of diamonds and gold there was need in the country's economy for the export of these things. Some of the animals were shot however, for the sheer joy and excitement of dealing out death by fine marksmanship. To seek refuge from the slayers the sadly thinned-out and daily imperilled game populations made their way north through thorny bushlands and stunted forests towards the Limpopo. Elephants left the *veld* and roamed the wastes of the Kalahari Desert, hoping to find safety there, only to be pursued and slaughtered by Boers and Bushmen alike. Areas of South Africa that were several times the size of Germany were practically denuded of wild life.

Sickened and appalled by this mass extermination on a nation-wide scale, the stern old Boer leader "Oom" Paul Kruger, himself a deadly shot and keen hunter, decided that the remnants of the game had to be saved for posterity. Refusing to bow to the storms of protest from his politically-powerful farmer country-men and at the grave risk to his position as "God-chosen" Boer patriarch, Kruger took up the cause of protection for the animals. In 1898 he gave up his own lands in the north-eastern Transvaal, persuaded some of his neighbours to do the same and gave to the country Africa's first game reserve.

This original, comparatively small, area was later enlarged to become the fine 8,000-square-mile Kruger National Park, 200 miles long and 40 miles wide, which begins south of the Limpopo and stretches to the south of the Oliphant and Sabi rivers to the Mozambique border.

The Park, where game rangers are armed with rifles against spear-and-snare poachers, has become world renowned. Its inhabitants include, among the larger antelope, tsessebe, blue wilde-beest and sleek sable whose horns are swept back proudly like an archer's bow; among the medium-sized antelope are mountain reedbuck and Limpopo bushbuck and among the small antelope grey duiker and Sharpe's grysbok. There are to be found, too, the African and Indian elephant, the Transvaal Burchell's zebra, the chacma baboon (enemy of the farmers since the settler days), and the grey-footed squirrel. Among the carnivora are kaffir cats, rusty genets, banded mongooses, Cape otters and lions, which frequently pad in single file alongside visitors' cars. The big cats even use the vehicles as cover when hunting and have been known to spring on to the bonnets and peer balefully but harmlessly in through the windscreen at the nervous occupants.

A friend of mine who was driving through the Park turned from talking to passengers in the back of his car just in time to brake to a stop under the spreadeagled forelegs of a giraffe. All the animals in the Park have right of way, and a giraffe can shatter a car's engine with a well-aimed "penalty kick".

Visitors are exhorted to travel very slowly, especially around corners, when in the Park's elephant country and not to try to pass cow elephants with young but to turn back as soon as possible or remain perfectly quiet until the elephants have gone. Tourists wishing to photograph bull elephants near the road are wisely advised to drive a little way past the animals before stopping the car and not to stop to take pictures while the animals are still ahead. Another golden rule they are given is: "Do not stop to photograph a herd of elephant cows and calves, but make haste to get away."

Everywhere there are signs warning that elephants are dangerous—"Olifante is gevaarlik".

Under the National Parks' Act No. 56 of 1926 it is an offence to:

Alight from a motor vehicle elsewhere than in a rest camp or picnic spot.

Drive elsewhere than on an authorized road.

Drive at a speed exceeding 25 m.p.h. on the roads and 10 m.p.h. in the rest camps.

Injure, feed or disturb any form of wild life.

Pull out, break or cut off or destroy any plant or tree.

Write any name, letter, figure, symbol, mark or sign on any object.

Throw out any burning object at any place where it may cause a fire.

Introduce into the Park any pets, whether domestic or non-domestic.

Be in possession of an unsealed weapon.

Pretoriuskop in the south-west corner of the Park is a model for camps in other parks in Africa. Summertime is lambing time, when Pretoriuskop is the haunt of a wide variety of game easily spotted against the vivid green background. And: "When the sun sinks slowly to the western horizon one becomes conscious of an uneasy silence, and as twilight gathers, tension mounts higher and higher until the descent of darkness suddenly alerts every beast of prey to his cunning nightly errand. In the next few hours death will strike swiftly at many places, but within the safety of the rest camps, by flickering fires and singing kettles—you must reach the camp before the gates close—only the roar of the animals beyond the fence provides a reminder of the drama outside."

Family groups of white rhino, rare in Africa since they were hunted out north of the Equator by nomadic tribes, live with little danger from poachers and other predators in reserves in Natal. Best-known of these reserves is tropically picturesque Hluhluwe where the white rhino, less fierce and more predictable than their lighter-in-weight black cousins, have become so docile and accustomed to man that African guides and visitors are able to walk up close to them in safety.

For some of South Africa's white rhino, Christmas, 1961, was hectic. They were shot with a drug-dart gun, hauled on to a truck and carted from the Native Reserve lands into which they had strayed to the Umfolosi and Nduma game reserves in Natal.

During this operation in the sweltering Mona River Valley Senior Game Ranger Ian Player spotted four square-lipped rhinos facing a group of snarling, half-starved African mongrels. The rhinos, a bull and three cows, trotted off in a temper until they deemed it safe to resume their grazing away from the dogs. Down wind, Ian stalked from bush to bush. Suddenly he stood up and, aiming at the 4,000-lb. bull, squeezed the trigger of his gun. With a "plop" a six-inch dart was buried deep in the animal's side. The bull and cows surged forward and Ian slipped behind an acacia tree as the rhinos thundered past. Darting out of hiding, he signalled to two horsemen to pursue the bull—because

Right : A running noose of wire, one of the most deadly of the poachers' traps.

Left : A young antelope killed by a poacher's snare of wire in Southern Rhodesia.

Right : This duiker was caught in a poacher's wire noose but was not moving fast enough to be killed. It might have strangled itself in efforts to escape, died from thirst or met its end from the poacher's spear. This animal was lucky ; game wardens found it and released it uninjured.

To obtain revenue tourism is encouraged. In the vast areas of the parks there must be bases where visitors can sleep in safety and cook where their fires will not create danger. Such bases are provided by *safari* lodges, of which that shown *above* is on the Ngorongoro Crater.

Left: Much of the "going" in the parks is rough; spare parts and plenty of petrol and drinking water are essential.

a rhino "shot" in this way will run for anything up to half an hour. After the drug had taken effect, the bull lay motionless and a lorry brought a crate up close to the inert beast. An antidote shot, which Ian gave to revive the rhino partially, worked almost immediately. After a few seconds the animal snorted, struggled forward and was bundled up a ramp into the crate by Ian and his assistants. Tall Zulu tribesmen crowded round with cries of amazement and unmistakable gestures which questioned the sanity of white men in wasting time and money protecting animals which the Zulus clearly felt should be tracked down, killed and eaten.

Some of the few elephant that remained in South Africa after the Boers' orgy of destruction were concentrated in the Addo district of the Cape near Port Elizabeth. They became a special breed, living in the jungle from which they would emerge all too frequently to pillage the surrounding orange groves and fruit farms. Angry farmers shot so many of the raiders that there were less than a dozen left when the Government stepped in and erected a stout and high, twelve-mile-long steel fence behind which the scared and evil-tempered survivors eventually settled down to breed in peace. Oranges, fed to them in barrel-loads, still remain the favourite delicacy of the Addo elephants.

South Africa, as if to redeem its early history of destruction, has long shown the way in game husbandry. Some ten years ago the Government was becoming increasingly worried over the scarcity of wild animals. As a result farms were established on which they could multiply without being preyed upon. To farmers who thereafter became interested in stocking game, animals were supplied; sometimes beasts were carried 1,000 miles or more from their normal habitat to their new homes, where they formed the nucleus of herds. In the Transvaal alone hundreds of farmers have made money by raising game commercially.

Some of the Government and municipal game farms are concentrating on building up the rarer species like the hartebeest and black wildebeest. Pretoria Municipality, for instance, has a

L

thriving game farm where animals are culled in the ordinary way and the meat is sold as biltong and venison on the local markets. The cost of the special jackal-proof fencing round the farm was met out of revenue from game-meat sales.

Throughout South Africa thousands of head are now harvested every year, the numbers being determined by regular inspections through which the maximums to be taken without reducing the basic herds are decided.

What began as experiments a decade ago are today an extremely important part of the Republic's agricultural and Nature conservation programme.

Game biltong has been outlawed in South Africa, except that which comes from farms where game are bred to supply venison and biltong to town markets. Accordingly, the prices of illicit game biltong have risen sharply (ordinary beef biltong, not considered as good as game biltong, sells from 9s. to 12s. 6d. a lb. in the Cape), and South African poachers have been shooting it out in a pitiless "biltong war" with camel-mounted members of the British Bechuanaland Police along the 1,000-mile northern border of the Protectorate. Poachers' trucks with game meat worth £8,000 from a single poaching expedition have been captured.

The Johannesburg *Sunday Times* of 13 May, 1962, reported: "Last month Major John Bowen, District Commissioner of Tsabong (in the south-western corner of Bechuanaland) fined two policemen and two farmers R200 (£100) each and confiscated their guns and ammunition. They had driven 40 miles into Bechuanaland on a poaching expedition from South-west Africa."

"To some poachers, the life of one policeman or game warden is disregarded as long as the body is not found before the vultures and hyenas have dealt with it." "In recent months there has been an increase in the number of poachers who fly into Bechuanaland from the Cape and Transvaal. They land on dry pans, shoot enough buck to fly out or, by low-flying, 'herd' the game down to the guns of friends waiting on the border."

*

Tanganyika

In August and September, 1961, the author
visited Arusha, Manyara National Park,
Ngorongoro Crater and Seringeti National
Park.

He tells of the annual migration from
Serengeti and its consequences; of the fight
against poaching; of the campaign by
Africans to convince the more primitive
tribesmen of the advantages of wild animal
conservation.

Chapter 21

FUNERAL PYRES

Fᴿᴱᴱ ᴛᴀɴɢᴀɴʏɪᴋᴀ is one of the poorest countries in modern Africa, but it has Serengeti. This vast and famous National Park contains the world's greatest and most spectacular concentration of plains game, such as wildebeest, zebra, gazelle, hartebeest and its cousin the topi, eland and giraffe. Serengeti is also renowned for its lion colonies which include some majestic, black-maned specimens. Prides of up to twenty lions moving swiftly and silently through the grass to the kill or lazing in the shade when the sun is high are not uncommon.

In the more wooded areas of the Park buffaloes roam in herds that often total several hundred beasts. On the granite outcrops of the *kopjes* that spring from the rolling parkland and acacia savannah of Serengeti can be seen that pert "Walt Disney" animal, the *klipspringer*, a small buck with outsize hooves developed for rock climbing, which poses on the rocks like a ballet dancer.

Tragically, the present boundaries of Serengeti National Park were drawn in such a way that 15,000 animals, mainly wildebeest and zebra, have to leave its protection each dry season. They provide teeming prey for poachers while on their way from the Central Province to the permanent water of Lake Victoria. The annual migration provides one of the most thrilling and remarkable sights in Africa as great herds of animals, nine or ten abreast and sometimes several miles long, move steadily westwards. Cripples and game too old to keep up get snatched by lion and other carnivore.

A hideous end, too, awaits many of the fit and fleet.

"I will show you the type of thing that goes on for seven months of the year," declared leathery, pint-sized Myles Turner, relentless enemy of the poachers and Deputy Chief Warden in Serengeti.

Rendered distinctive by his twelve-year-old bush hat of which the rotting crown was stitched with red thread, ex-hunter Myles was to lead us on day-long anti-poaching raids outside the boundaries of the Park. His lieutenants were Assistant Warden Gordon Poolman and an impressive pipe-puffing African Mr. Aloysius Mlay, who proudly wore the drab-green bush kit and deer stalker "uniform "of one of his country's first non-White game wardens.

When Mr. Mlay ,who speaks English fluently and flamboyantly, is not chasing poachers or being buried in his office under a shower of official forms, he tours the African villages preaching to chiefs and other tribesmen about game conservation and the need for national parks. His appointment is the prelude to eventual full control of the animal sanctuaries in Tanganyika by Africans, such as himself, dedicated to saving the wild life from the ruthless predators among his people.

In some of the villages visited during his tours this fervent and vital pioneer has audiences of more than 300 people. To his fellow Africans he says: "Game is Tanganyika's richest asset, and indiscriminate killing is both wrong and harmful to the economy of our new African nation. Tanganyika is one of the few countries in the world where wild life is plentiful. The Tanganyika national parks, which belong to the people of our country, are charged with the preservation of this great asset. Our country has three great problems to solve, namely Poverty, Ignorance and Disease. Our Government is pledged to follow up any means available to combat one or all of them. Tanganyika derives many benefits from wild game. For the last five years she received well over £703,000 from the sale of licences and of Government trophies such as ivory, rhino horns and leopard skins. Over and above this, larger amounts of money went into the pockets of our people from tourists visiting the country to see our wild game in the national parks. While in Tanganyika they spend their money in buying food and drink and paying for their accommodation, transport and guides.

"It is estimated that Tanganyika receives well over £2,000,000 every year from tourists. The more money our Government gets from this source the less taxes we will be asked to pay. The Government imposes taxes because it needs money to pay for the various services for the welfare of the people of the country. Therefore, it is to our advantage to help the national parks in carrying out their work in preserving wild game.

"Again, the more tourists that come to Tanganyika to see our wild life, the more widely will the country's potentials be known in the outside world. People come to Tanganyika to see our wild game because there is little or none in their own countries. It has been killed off. We must, therefore, preserve our wild game for our children and grandchildren and for the people of other countries to come to see.

"The wild life in our national parks helps to defeat one of our big enemies, poverty, by bringing money to our Government and our people. And to help to feed our people there is a scheme now being studied by expert scientists. This is game cropping. When completed it will be possible to distribute meat to the people through their chiefs and this will help defeat another enemy of Tanganyika, malnutrition."

Typical of the questions Mr. Mlay is asked is why are arrested poachers taken away to the courts without their relatives being informed through the chief—because "this is a hardship to their families who sometimes think that their husbands and fathers have been lost".

To this he replies sternly: "Any person who breaks the laws of the country must be taken to a competent court at the earliest opportunity. We will not help law breakers. When the head of a family does not obey the laws of a country he forfeits our sympathy. You yourselves do not like to sympathize with thieves."

To requests for the return of sections of national park land to the tribes Mr. Mlay is authorized to answer with a curt "No". He adds: "Our Government will not entertain the idea of giving away pieces of the national parks by changing the boundaries here and there to calm frivolous demands. It is in the minds of some leaders in Tanganyika to expand the parks rather than to constrict them."

★   ★   ★

Our expedition, with armed African game wardens, Land-Rovers and a lorry set off. After an hour's drive outside the park we were in a valley on the main migration route of game where the animals run the gauntlet of hordes of poachers. Under a tree by a waterhole we found the first loop snare of unbreakable steel wire, strong enough to hold a lion. Such wire frequently partially severs the trapped animal's head as it struggles to free itself. The snare was quickly torn down and tossed into the back of the lorry by Gordon Poolman. He told me of a pursued poacher who jumped into a small lake in the district and hid under the water lilies. "We just waited quietly until he came choking to the surface, then we nabbed him."

The snares were thick in the trees. While each one was being dismantled, there was the constant menace of lurking aggressive tribesmen waiting to attack us with a shower of poisoned arrows from the bushes around.

Vultures led us to our first poachers' hide-out in a thicket in the Sumfuji Basin. Of the five African killers who fled from the camp, in which they had lived in tiny grass huts, two were caught by tracking. The camp was littered with wire snares and poisoned arrows. Strips of topi, zebra, wildebeest and impala meat were strung out to dry on poles among the trees. In one corner were stacked the legs, heads, horns and skins of some fifteen animals slaughtered by the poachers.

"Carriers come in on bicycles to take the dried or smoked meat to the villages where it fetches about three shillings an 18-inch-square strip," said Mr. Mlay as he examined a sheaf of metal-tipped spears used by the poachers to kill animals found still alive in the snares. The poison usually does not contaminate the meat because a small square of flesh where the arrow strikes is cut out of the body with the poacher's knives.

"They also occasionally dig pits for lion, zebra, impala—anything," Myles Turner told me. "We do not begrudge the hungry man a buck or two. But tons and tons of meat are going out regularly. It is wholesale slaughter, and the beginning of the end of the migratory Serengeti game unless this ghastly trade is stopped."

When the dried meat had been loaded on to the lorry (some of it is used as evidence and the rest given away to law-abiding tribesmen), the other ghastly remains of the animals and their skins were flung into the grass hut which was set on fire with a single match and the entire thicket camp went up in a fierce blaze.

Driving to the next suspect thicket, Myles stopped by a zebra which had died in a snare. In a day it had been eaten to a skeleton by vultures and hyenas.

The second camp, three miles from the first, was larger and contained forty head of slaughtered game. The inhabitants, warned of our approach on the weird and silent jungle grapevine, had disappeared. They had left behind ample evidence of their grim trade, and the still-warm gourd pipes in which most poachers smoke *dagga* weed (*hashish*) to give them courage for the often hazardous encounters with their victims. There was fresh blood on the hunters' spears leaning against the side of the two grass huts which were also set on fire before we moved on.

"To think that some Africans are now poaching zebra and other game with Land-Rovers and shotguns," said Myles grimly. "They are now in and out of an area before we have a chance to spot and catch them."

The third thicket camp we discovered hid four "Beehive" huts and the carcasses, haunches and heads of game killed the day before with ancient muskets, spears, bows and arrows and wire snares. Flies crawled everywhere and the stench was nauseating.

This hide also was set ablaze, and marabou storks waited in trees to enter the smouldering camp for a peck of charred meat. We captured fifteen poachers that day, including a 12-year-old boy. The men were later convicted and each sentenced to six months' imprisonment.

Shortly before our trip, Myles, in his unceasing battle, turned out with his men and in one day burnt down seventeen camps, some containing up to ten huts, and captured sixty-five tons of dried and fresh meat.

"Vanishing game all right," he remarked savagely. "Prison is no deterrent. We have got to turn on the heat from the top and impose collective fines."

With the grisly picture of the poachers' carnage vivid in the mind's eye, few words were exchanged between us on the journey back into the Serengeti Park. With the Land-Rover throwing up heavy spurts of grey dust, clouds of sand-grouse exploded into the dying sun at our approach.

Then suddenly, at a shout from Gordon Poolman, the African driver stamped on the brakes.

'Look," shouted Gordon pointing to a thorn tree a hundred yards off the road. "In that branch to the right." We could see nothing but trees and earth and sky. Yet when we lurched over the *veld* and stopped beneath the tree I found the yellow-green eyes of a young leopard boring into mine from six feet above. He was sprawled languidly in a fork, like the lions which also "roost" in trees in Serengeti, but the rippling muscles on his magnificent coat showed that he was tensed and ready to spring. Eventually, bored with our company in the familiar box on wheels, he turned his gaze to a nearby herd of gazelle in anticipation of an evening kill.

Vultures, officially protected as the garbage birds of the jungle and *veld*, fought over the remains of a topi, another leopard victim, beneath a neighbouring tree while others lined the branches, waiting to join in the macabre scramble.

With but two miles to go before reaching Seronera Tourists'

Camp, we stopped within stroking distance of a pride of lion, one of which was chewing contentedly on a bicycle tyre. Two months before a lion had snatched a White visitor from his tent at Seronera and mauled him to death. We were unable, however, to solve the riddle of the source of that bicycle tyre. As we drove on a baboon posed among the sunlit foliage looked for all the world like a Japanese print.

We drove on to Myles Turner's house for gin and orange sundowners served by his attractive wife, whose charm hides her ever-present, gnawing fear that in Myles's ruthless war on the poachers they will one day take deadly revenge with poisoned arrows on their two children, three-year old Lynda Jane and baby Michael. It is the measure of her courage that she retains her place at her husband's side and that Serengeti remains her home.

Myles, who is today one of the best-known wardens in Africa, was born at Low Row in Cumberland in 1921 and came to Kenya at the age of three when his father began a farming venture in the Colony. During the war he served in Africa and abroad in an armoured-car unit of the East African Reconnaissance Squadron. After the war he became a white hunter, working first for the Kenya Game Department on control shooting and later for a large Nairobi firm which organized big game *safaris* for rich sportsmen. In 1956, when he had "shot all the animals I ever wanted to", Myles successfully applied for a job as a warden in Serengeti and has been there—"working like a slave", as his many friends in the "game game" will tell you—ever since.

Myles has two hobbies. They are big-game fishing off the coast in the Indian Ocean and an intensive and sustained interest in all forms of bull-fighting. He has seen one bull-fight—in Spain in 1954—but the shelves in his lounge at Seronera are crammed with, to use his own words, "everything that has ever been written about bull-fighting". He is, of course, a Hemingway fan. It was Hemingway who first aroused Myles's almost fanatical interest in all aspects of the bull-ring by his descriptions of a study in death—"and death's the only thing in life".

Myles's albums at the house contain some of the finest ground and aerial photographs ever taken of wildebeest and zebra migrating across the game plains. In some shots lions making kills are seen as "islands" among the black-massed tens of thousands.

He delved into a drawer of his writing-desk and tossed over a report on poaching which he had written to the trustees of the Park a few weeks before.

"Unless something is done immediately," he warned, "our great migratory herds are doomed *within a decade or less* and the smoke from the burning camps can be taken as the first funeral pyres of the fabulous game of Serengeti."

Said Myles: "I have never written anything with greater force or sincerity . . . Come over to my camp office."

It was cluttered with poachers' snares, poisoned arrows, bows with the strings made from animal sinews, cobras and other snakes pickled in bottles, and official handbooks.

"Peak months for poaching," he said, "are June to December when it is dry, and the game are concentrated round the permanent water. Poaching eases off when the rains come and the game disperses."

In 1957 there were 108 convictions for poaching in the Serengeti area, 89 in 1958, 115 in 1959 and 116 in 1960. Yet in only the first six months of 1961 the convictions shot up to 162 and looked like trebling the 1957 figure.

"And we have only thirty rangers, out-numbered and over-worked, to patrol 6,000 square miles," added Myles.

Steel cable used for snares is stolen in thousands of feet—and later cut up into six-foot lengths—from diamond and gold mines near the Park, and some 9,000 snares had been destroyed by wardens and rangers during the previous five years. This monumental figure represents but a small proportion of the snares which were set, remained undiscovered, and took their toll in torture and death.

"Snares are as effective as an atom bomb in wiping out game," said Myles who at that time was learning to fly a light aircraft in order to step up his campaign against the poachers. "It's now up to the African leaders to solve the problem. One important step would be for them to follow the practice in Kenya and ban the use of arrow poison. Poisoned arrows are allowed in Tanganyika for self-defence and crop protection. Practically all the murders here are done with arrows tipped with poison. Perhaps we may get it prohibited on that score. And I'd like to see very heavy penalties for anyone found in the bush with lengths of steel wire in his possession."

Adding almost crushing weight to their set-backs and difficulties in the struggle, Myles and his men find that motorized poaching is increasing alarmingly. Any Game Ranger who tries to interfere is liable to be run down by the poachers. Of course if they are caught the Land-Rovers or lorries used are confiscated, but this is not proving to be an adequate deterrent. Not all the poachers are Africans. There are some Europeans and Asians, too.

These well-organized professional butchers are able to kill their prey with rifles or shotguns and sell the meat—all in one day!

Chapter 22

"JUDGEMENT WILL BE HARSH"

IT had been a glorious and memorable day. We had been out with Gordon Poolman, watching lion, leopard and an occasional cheetah loping across the grasslands, each with their own poetic metre of motion. Only one incident had marred our trip. This was the discovery of a sick young wildebeest, panting and shuddering on the ground. It had been abandoned by the herd. Death was but a matter of hours away; there was nothing in this case that Gordon could do to keep the flame of existence flickering.

Now the moon was a silver sickle above Seronera and in the cool of the evening John S. Owen, shaggy, keen-eyed Director of Tanganyika National Parks, had drawn up folding canvas chairs round a stone bird-bath in front of the living quarters to talk of his work. He set his whisky and soda down on the grass and remarked quietly, "The leaders of this country are well aware of the necessity to conserve wild life . . . they are sympathetic, but in any democratic country you cannot disregard public opinion."

Understandably, he said, the majority of the general public, in fact, the tribesmen, in Tanganyika lagged farther behind the Government on the question of game than on any other matter. That was not surprising. The tribesmen were struggling to scrape a bare living from the soil and seldom took a long-term view.

"After all, it is only very recently that the more advanced nations have themselves woken up to the need for faunal conservation. And then only after they had destroyed all, or all but a fragment, of what they had to conserve."

There were special factors affecting African public opinion in Tanganyika and elsewhere as regards wild animals. For centuries the African depended on hunting for an important and most palatable part of his diet. Before the coming of the White man and his destructive new methods of killing, man and animals lived in balance. Hunting was a legitimate and honourable activity which had the full support of tribal tradition behind it. Since the White man came the African has seen him exterminate the game over large areas, partly for food, partly for sport, partly for gain and partly to protect his farms from depredation and competitive grazing. The African did not see why he should be stopped by the White man from doing the same.

"For instance, he fails to understand the equity of a law which sentences him to a heavy term of imprisonment for killing an animal for food on his traditional tribal hunting grounds while it allows a visiting White man to shoot a number of beasts on his land. For this and other reasons, African thinking on game preservation is often coloured by the racial issue."

There was a fear in some parts of Africa that the Africans on obtaining their freedom would kill all the game merely to "hit back at the Whites".

Mr. Owen dropped another cube of ice into his glass and went on to tell me a comforting story. Two or three chiefs, he said, had been agitating to take over sections of outer Serengeti for their people and cattle, but, after visiting the Park, an African M.P. had told them sharply that there was no question of them being allowed to take "bites" out of the Park and if they persisted in their demands they would be moved back from its borders.

A propaganda campaign among Africans had been launched with the making of a £3,000, half-hour film, the first of several to be produced in Swahili illustrating the value and purpose of National Parks. To the same end African lecturers had toured schools, community centres, agricultural shows and gatherings.

Through the efforts of Dr. Bernhard Grzimek, Curator of the Frankfurt Zoo and author of the book *Serengeti Shall Not Die*, the Zoological Society of Frankfurt had donated supplies of coloured posters showing an African family looking at an elephant, zebra and impala and bearing the words in Swahili: "The whole world envies our National Parks. We must be proud of them". (*Ulimwenguni kote wanatami* National Parks *zetu. Lazima Tujivunie.* Another poster was being prepared with the slogan, "Our National Parks bring good money into Tanganyika—preserve them."

Regular visits of chiefs and parties of school children were being made to the parks, and money prizes awarded to the children for the best essays on their trips.

Mr. Owen tossed over the pages of some typical essays.

"What country in the world has the wealth of the type we Africans have inherited?" wrote one boy. "What country has rhinos, lions, giraffes and zebra. None but our Africa. The National Parks are part of our land where game animals can be safeguarded, where they hurt no one. On the contrary, so that they may always be there so that we may see them—we and our grandchildren too—we have inherited something great which draws the eyes of the whole world. Other lands cannot but be jealous of us and our wealth."

And another: "Visitors from all parts of the world come to tour our land so that they can see our wealth—the animals. If they come, then they will spend much money in our country, money which can profit every person in the country. And if visitors come from various countries, must we not get a greater understanding with them. Thus we shall build up friendships with other nations, exchange views and assist one another. Then these visitors will understand our difficulties and see what assistance we need. Tanganyika can get as good a name in the world for its National Parks as it has already got for its constitutional development. In other lands, America for example, hunters in the past destroyed almost all the animals and later on people bitterly regretted this. What human being is able to create new animals. Let us not come to regret. Let us safeguard our wealth."

The multi-racial trustees of Tanganyika National Parks say they are having to operate on a shoe string in seeing that the game of the country survives the impact of Western civilization. Help from international sources is difficult to get because wild life is not a factor in the cold war and had little propaganda value.

"The need is urgent if our plans are to have any chance of success," declare the trustees in an appeal for funds. "Events in Africa are moving very fast. A high proportion of the larger species of animals are now in real and immediate danger of extinction within the next generation. Once they are gone, they are gone for ever. The judgement of posterity on us will be harsh if we allow the wanton destruction of so much beauty and grace. Unless the world does something effective at once, the rhino, kudu, lion and giraffe will very shortly join the Great Auk in the limbo of animals that man has wiped from the face of the earth. And the elephant, the gazelle and all the others will follow not long after."

Mr. Owen stood up and gathered his papers together. "The United Nations will send us experts," he said. "But we want bullets in the form of money, not staff officers. We know how to fight the battle."

To the majority of rural Africans the elephant is a dangerous agricultural pest which should be inside every tribesman's

In Tsavo West Royal National Park Warden "Tuffy" Marshall put down boreholes and ran pipelines to supply artificial waterholes like that *above*. (See page 54.) Each pool can meet the needs of between forty and fifty elephants a day. On one occasion when the supply to the pool failed elephant members of the "Kayabondo Drinking Club" tore up the earth and damaged the supply pipe in their search for water.

Left: A young bull elephant has emerged from the bush and entwined trunks with a young cow. The photograph was taken in the Wankie Game Reserve in Southern Rhodesia.

Left: Peter Johnstone writes: "I built two hides one behind the other. I sat in the front one; in the hide behind I placed my European hunter with the camera. A lone kudu bull arrived and must have been very thirsty because it was not cautious. My hunter tried to take the picture as I fired, but got it only after the animal had fallen."

Above: Though to the human eye this "hide" bears obvious signs of man's handiwork, to the animals it is merely an unmoving object spelling no threat. Within it the rifleman can sit undetected.

Below: Though one animal is dead the slight noise from the silenced rifle has not frightened others away from the water.

stomach; every lion is a savage killer of man and stock, and the wildebeest an unwelcome competitor for sparse grazing. They are puzzled by the mystical and romantic regard of others for wild animals.

It is gratifying to record that Tanganyika is comparatively far ahead in its efforts to convince the mass of Africans—a truly monumental task—that animals in parks and reserves can be more use to them alive than dead, that the legacy of wild game can be made to earn its keep and that money necessary to preserve them is not always better spent on more schools and doctors.

Chapter 23

THE TORCH

THE little town of Arusha in northern Tanganyika lies, white-washed and sun-drenched, at the foot of towering Mount Meru. For its meagre fame it used to rely on periodic visits of Hollywood film units on African location and a claim to be the half-way point between Cairo and the Cape.

Then, in September 1961, it became a landmark in the history of wild-life preservation. It was the venue of the greatest assembly of international experts on African fauna and flora ever to meet on African soil. The clumsily grandiose title of their conference was "The Symposium on the Conservation of Nature and Natural Resources in Modern African States". Whittled down to single-breath size by its organizers, the Commission for Technical Co-operation South of the Sahara and the International Union for the Conservation of Nature and Natural Resources in collaboration with Unesco and F.A.O., it became simply "African Special Project".

The purpose of the conference was to discuss, and to draw the attention of the world to, the urgent problem of finding ways and means of halting the drain on the African continent's wild life and on the habitat upon which it depends. It aimed to bring governments of modern African states face-to-face with their responsibilities in the maintenance and development of natural resources.

Black, white and brown delegates were fervently united in their desire to find a solution to the overall problem of game conservation. To this league of nations to save the animal world came Western-clothed African cabinet ministers from newly independent African countries and specialists from America, Belgium, Britain, the Sudan, West Germany and the Central African Federation. Blanket-robed chiefs mingled with English scientists and European game experts.

No African leader from Kenya attended; the general feeling at the conference was that they were too embroiled in the settling of political differences to be interested at that time in the fate of the game herds or in how best to preserve Africa as a haven for wild life in its natural setting.

Delegates who travelled by road to Arusha from Nairobi saw many stark reminders of the tragedy with which they had to grapple. Throughout the 180-mile journey the bleached skeletons of game animals, victims of drought, famine and disease, lay on either side of the tarmac.

In a forceful speech before opening the conference, the Governor of Tanganyika, Sir Richard Turnbull, said that it was not enough to condemn poaching, to acclaim tourism and to leave it at that. They had to apply their education, their propaganda, their information services and their persuasive powers not merely to the conservation of game but to the conservation of the habitat upon which the game depended.

"To my mind what is at stake is something far more fundamental than the preservation of wild animals," declared Sir Richard. "It is the continuance in being of a special form of natural resource which, once lost, can never be replaced, but which, if conserved, can be a permanent and self-renewing asset. It is a form of natural resource infinitely more precious than gold or diamonds; for once you have extracted the diamond from the soil, or wrested the gold from the ore in which it lies, the natural resources of the country have been to that extent depleted. It is true that you can convert the wealth that is created into social services; but the diamond and the gold have gone, and have gone for good. You can't breed diamonds from diamonds, or cause gold to regenerate itself. But the fauna and flora of a country, if properly managed and conserved, can be an increasing and constantly renewable source of wealth as well as being a refreshment to the spirit. Further, a country can survive without mineral resources but deprived of its cover of vegetation, it will unfailingly perish."

The matter of the preservation of the habitat was as important to man as it was to wild life. For the precarious foothold that man maintained of the outer integument of his planet depended primarily on two things; on keeping in place the soils which were the source of their food, and on preserving the vegetational cover without which the soils would be wasted or blown away. The vegetational cover depended upon the soils, and the soils upon the vegetational cover.

"One would have thought that since man's present comfort and future survival so hang upon the proper treatment of his fields, his pastures and his forests—for it is upon these that he chiefly relies for the maintenance of those climatic limits outside which he cannot exist—he would do his best to cherish and protect them. That he seems to be steadily bent on their destruction is one of the chief reasons of our being here today.

"The future of this vegetational cover is the future not only of game but of man, and to the extent that we harm it or allow it to be harmed, so will the future of man and of game be put in jeopardy.

"Nobody who has worked in the field in the drier parts of Africa can fail to have been appalled by the effect upon man's habitat of overcropping, over-grazing and fire. The process is plain for all to see; it starts with a simple gullying, proceeds to widespread sheet erosion, and ends with the country stripped of its previously fertile soils and reduced to bare rocks and shifting sand dunes; and all this through the activities of man "

The "much maligned" Masai had a champion at the conference in Mr. H. A. Fosbrooke, Chairman of the Ngorongoro Conservation Authority, who said they were among the best friends of game. Where the Masai had retained the land against alien encroachment—African and European—the game had remained. Where the Masai had lost their land, teeming game life had disappeared. An equally good friend of the game, he said, was the tsetse fly, keeping humans and livestock at bay.

It was no good educating governments to conserve game. The electorate must also be persuaded.

On poaching, Mr. Fosbrooke said it was more important to take action against illicit traders than against poachers themselves. The export of game trophies and by-products needed to be controlled.

Mr. L. H. Brown, Acting Director of Kenya's Agricultural Department, said in a paper: "Wild animals in the present conditions of an exploding population in the world can scarcely hope to retain any large area of land in the face of possible competition from intensive agriculture. But it would appear to be irrational and irresponsible to jeopardize the natural resource represented by game, either as a source of protein or as a tourist attraction, for the sake of primitive pastoralism or of organized capitalist ranching. Necessary reductions in domestic stock will improve rather than harm pastoralists by preventing them from destroying land and themselves as they have been doing for centuries."

Mr. R. Knobel, Director of South Africa's National Parks, told the conference that politicians were seeking human and not animal votes and if forced to choose would always favour humans. There was a limit to land which could be set aside, but parks must be big enough to form separate units without animals encroaching on land outside.

Professor Huxley said Africans must learn to educate Africans on the importance of wild life. He pointed out that in developed countries schemes which were regarded as of value to the population as a whole were subsidized by governments.

Delegates listened in grim and shocked silence as Colonel Cowie, Director of Kenya's Royal National Parks, launched a bitter attack on his government for what he described as its "two-faced" game policy which was making the protectors of wild life powerless to prevent suffering and destruction.

"The situation in Kenya calls for the greatest possible assistance," he said. "It is more than unfortunate that none of the Kenya African political leaders has found it possible to attend this conference, and that in itself is significant of the attitude in Kenya towards the conservation of natural resources. I therefore feel compelled to inform all of you of the disastrous situation in regard to preservation of wild life and its habitat which has now been reached in Kenya.

"In my opinion, for the past few years the Kenya Government has betrayed the cause of conservation. It amounts to a gigantic hoax. On the one hand there have been Government statements of game policy, approved by the Legislature, confirming the Government's intention to preserve wild life and to recognize its full value to the economy of the country in a pattern of proper land-use planning. But, on the other hand, there have been no effective steps taken to implement this policy, or to find the money necessary to do so. It amounts to lip service merely to beguile the architects of the policy and future governments. Kenya, although the pioneer of national parks in East Africa, is now lagging far behind its neighbours in all these spheres of achievement."

Colonel Cowie revealed that the annual Kenya Government grant for national parks had been cut by £10,000. No assistance in kind had been granted, such as the exemption of Customs duty as in Tanganyika or the free employment of prison labour. Thus, the Kenya Government had brought national parks and the Game Department to a point of bankruptcy, and had allowed thousands of cattle to enter and plunder the western section of Tsavo Park.

Colonel Cowie ended with an impassioned appeal to the delegates: "On behalf of the animals I have spent most of my life trying to protect, I put forward an S O S—and an urgent S O S—from the dying plains of Kenya."

He refrained from adding, as I knew he had felt in a passing spasm of abject despair, "Why not shoot the lot and have done with it."

Professor Huxley has since stated that during the conference there was much pessimism and discouragement to set against hope. Yet he and all his fellow delegates agreed that a torch lit by the Tanganyika Government and carried into the school-hall conference dispelled the crowding shadows that day. Accepting trusteeship of the country's wild life and responsibility for its preservation in a manifesto believed to be the first of its kind in the history of the world, the Government pledged: "We solemnly declare that we will do everything in our power to make sure that our children's grandchildren will be able to enjoy this rich and precious inheritance. The survival of our wild life is a matter of grave concern to all of us in Africa. These wild creatures are not only important as a source of wonder and inspiration, but are an integral part of our natural resources and of our future livelihood and well-being. Conservation of wild life and wild places calls for specialist knowledge, trained manpower and money. We look to other nations to co-operate in this important task—the success or failure of which not only affects the continent of Africa but the rest of the world as well."

Before the Arusha conference broke up we visited the near-by Ngorongoro Crater, a basin fifteen miles across set in a volcanic massif that had been excised—not without considerable controversy—from the Serengeti. It had become a controlled area to enable the Masai to graze their cattle there and compete for diminishing waterholes while at the same time the wild animals were, in theory, unmolested.

Rocking perilously on the stony, twisting road from which, to the left, there was an awesome drop, we drove down the 2,500-ft.

escarpment in a Land-Rover into the great amphitheatre of the crater where herds of Masai cattle in their hundreds were drab and lethargic intruders in a thrilling, natural "circus" of lion, leopard, rhino, elephant, buffalo, cheetah, baboon, zebra and gazelles.

Perched 7,800 ft. above sea-level in a setting of scenic grandeur that is unexcelled, Ngorongoro, its floor once a lush meadow dotted with pools and criss-crossed with broad streams, is the second largest crater on earth and has been described by Dr. Grzimek as "the largest zoo in the world". Just over fifty years ago there were 24,000 head of zebra and wildebeest alone on the Ngorongoro stage. Today it is estimated there are only 8,000 wild animals of all species there.

Apart from bringing increasing numbers of cattle into the crater itself, the Masai have invaded the forests on the rim. In a typically shrinking wallow on the scorched, close-cropped crater floor we found a wounded female hippo with gaping gashes on her flanks caused by the spears of the hunters.

Professor Ritchie Calder, a British delegate, told how his party met a wounded rhino which no one dared to approach. In its side was a Masai spear with which it had been stabbed nine hours before.

"The game wardens and the indignant visitors cross-examined the Masai about this apparently wanton act. The chief answered with quiet dignity. The rhino, he said, had attacked the herd of cattle, killing four, and his young men, with their long spears, had come to the defence of the herd. They would have despised themselves as cowards had they done less. The Masai, the chief said firmly, did not kill wild game either for meat or for profit. They did not traffic as other tribes and non-Africans did in ivory and rhino horn. They only protected their cattle."

There had been widespread killings of rhino in the Ngorongoro area and, despite the chief's protestation, there were guilty men among the Masai who had struck down the animals not in self-defence or to protect the cattle but to sell the horns. The Tanganyika Government was offering £500 reward to anyone whose information led to the conviction of rhino poachers and middle-men.

The neighbouring crater of Lemagrut had been made bare and arid by over-grazing and fire.

"If cattle are allowed to continue to graze on the forest slopes and rim of Ngorongoro, it will soon become as barren," said Sir Richard Turnbull. "There will be habitat for neither game nor cattle nor, in the end, for man himself. Within the next five years there will have to be an adjustment of the normal Masai grazing cycle if Ngorongoro is to be saved. Alternative grazing areas will have to be found and supplied with water. Piped water seems the most satisfactory solution. A special Masai development plan may well be required. The Masai for their part must overcome their innate conservatism and recognize the inevitability of some such changes as these. They will have to accept that forest grazing is no longer available to them, and be prepared to adopt a kind of range management that is best suited to the physical conditions and carrying capacity of the land.

"The Government is trying to introduce some system that will enlist full co-operation and the confidence of the Tanganyika Masai, and will at the same time ensure conservation both of the game and of the habitat.

"The prospects of peaceful co-existence between the Masai and the game are good. The general attitude of the small African farmer to game, however, is not a particularly sympathetic one. This is not because he is a brutal, bloodthirsty character, but because he is fighting a desperate battle with harsh and grudging soil."

It was time to leave the crater and return to Arusha. I glanced back as the African driver of the Land-Rover pressed the starter button. With shrill cries and brandishing sticks, the red Masai tribesmen urged on their bunches of cattle towards the villages of huddled, box-like mud huts and clouds of dust—the dead earth—screened the setting sun.

SECTION EIGHT

*

Mozambique

"We try our best—but there are poachers
everywhere in Africa...."

Chapter 24

LIONS ARE CHEAP

IN his crumpled gold-braided uniform the swarthy, corpulent
Portuguese immigration officer at the Mozambique border post
oozed goodwill. Formalities over and with the prospect of an
obviously badly needed *siesta* in view he chatted proudly in
broken English of the "perils" of the night-long hunting expedition he had completed before coming on duty at daylight.

This, it appeared, had been a daring and exciting affair during
which any animal spotted and held in the glare of a spotlight
clamped to the *safari* truck manned by himself and his companions
was lucky if it escaped a hail of bullets. The rambling story of the
little official's *bushveld* "triumphs" was a nauseating and depressing introduction to this Portuguese East African territory.

Mozambique, like Angola in West Africa, is a province of the
Portuguese homeland. During my travels I had heard horrible
stories of a callous indifference there to the survival of wild life
when pounds or dollars were produced in thick wads as the price
of blindness to wholesale killings. When in Beira I tried to get to
the truth about them. There were language difficulties, of course;
even allowing for that Government officials were reticent or
nervously evasive when confronted with allegations by non-
Portuguese animal lovers and big game enthusiasts who had
visited Mozambique. They had claimed the elephants in the
territory are doomed as the result of widespread poaching,
trapping and an excess of legal and illegal hunting. The officials
agreed that elephant and rhino were the main targets but added
that Mozambique still had "far too many elephant". Asked
whether there were nightly mass killings of buffalo by biltong
hunters, the bland answer was: "That is a side issue of the trade in
ivory and rhino horns."

Another charge is that in Mozambique the game rangers are easily bribed to condone the illegal killing of animals. The reply, with a shrug of the shoulder, to this: "African game rangers are unreliable."

The response of the officials, as is obvious, was neither rewarding nor particularly illuminating. One of them protested: "Senhor, we try our best, but it is such a big country. After all, there is poaching everywhere in Africa."

It had also been claimed that licences for shooting are freely granted in the territory if bribes are offered to the right individuals. This may or may not be true. It is, however, a fact that these licences can be obtained at post offices and police stations in remote areas; it is also true that the licences cover a generous range of big and small game and are relatively cheap.

For instance, for $150 (£90) a visiting *safari* client can shoot: one buffalo, one zebra, two haartebeest, one wildebeest, two water buck, one impala, two reed buck, one crocodile, four wild pigs, five buck and two bush buck.

If these are not enough to satisfy the hunting instincts of one man, supplementary licence coupons are granted on the following scale:

one elephant $170; two buffaloes $13·50 each; one kudu $13·50; one hippo $17·70; two zebra $13·55 each; one nyala $17·00; one eland $27·00.

Surprisingly cheapest, and at the bottom of the list, are lion and leopard. It costs only $13·50 to bag a leopard and $12·00 for a lion. These low charges are something of a mystery for lion and leopard remain among the most coveted trophies. Perhaps they are offered as an incentive to visitors to prolong their stay. *Tourismo*, the Government's travel service, big game hunting and photographic *safari* quotations for 1962 for one client are:

$1,500 for a fortnight; $2,000 for three weeks; $2,500 for thirty days.

These charges include the services of an experienced white hunter, African gun bearers, trackers, skinners and personal servants, full camp equipment and meals, a hunting car and the treatment and care of trophies during the *safari*. Extras include the costs of the hunting licence and supplementary coupons and the packing and shipping of the trophies. A total of 500 rounds of ammunition may be imported by each licence holder, who is allowed one shotgun, one pistol and three rifles. Extra ammunition can be obtained easily in Beira. The hunting season in Mozambique opens on 1 May and closes on 31 December. It is clear that even at Government level, and taking only official tourist documents as a guide, widespread shooting on a generous scale is fostered and encouraged in Mozambique as a lucrative source of revenue.

Whatever the position, legal or illegal, outside, the territory's national park of Gorongosa, ninety-seven miles from Beira and covering some 2,000 square miles, remains, under its Portuguese game warden, a model sanctuary for animals of all types which are more numerous, perhaps, than in any other park of its size in Africa. The only rest camp in Gorongosa is Chitengo, situated between the Pungwe and Urema rivers. This consists of a restaurant building with bungalows and rondavels fitted out with running water, electric light, inner-spring mattresses and shower-baths—all in the midst of wild bush country and with tea brought to one's bedside at sunrise. The camp can cater for up to eighty persons at a time.

From Chitengo the visitor travels across a vast plain to see teeming herds of buffalo, zebra, wildebeest, waterbuck and impala, and then in to the forests where families of elephant browse. Along a bank of the river flamingoes, pelicans, storks and other gloriously-plumaged wild birds mingle with the crocodiles and colonies of hippo.

Gorongosa has often been called, with typical travel agent's licence, "a photographer's Paradise". In one startling respect it certainly is.

The rest camp of Gorongosa which existed before Chitengo was built consisted of brick bungalows and was situated near the Sungu River. Now it has been taken over by the Park's lion population. It is not unusual to find a litter of cubs sleeping on a porch in the sunshine while their parents peer out of a window, forepaws resting on the sill. As I cruised past one crumbling bunga-low in the Land-Rover there was a shattering roar, and an old lion which obviously regarded the main bedroom as his exclusive domain came bounding out like a huge shaggy dog chasing off the postman! Here can be taken still and movie camera shots the like of which so far as I know can be obtained in no other game reserve in all Africa.

SECTION NINE

*

Man:
Enemy and (?) Preserver

In a general summary of factors impinging on the wild animals of Africa, some of the circumstances affecting Man himself have important roles. Superstition and politics, land hunger and economics, indifference, selfishness and ignorance all play their part. The damage being done is enormous. But there is a reverse side to the coin. Economics (with some help from the tourist trade) and pride of possession (where it can be engendered) will be major factors on the side of conservation. Yet, without stimulus the total effect may be only to slow down slightly the rate of extermination. In the following pages some of the conflicting factors are outlined.

Right: Taken in Bungoro, Uganda, this photograph shows a termanalia tree which has been barked by elephants rubbing against it to rid themselves of parasites. The tree will soon die. Though wild animals do a little damage to vegetation it is not likely to lead to erosion of the soil. Domesticated cattle, sheep and goats on the other hand strip vegetation.

Below: Cattle are indiscriminate grazers, leaving only clumps of rank grass behind. Often this grass is burnt to bring up a fresh bite. Trees are destroyed in the fires and eventually, neither cattle nor wild beast can live off what soon becomes a dust bowl. This picture shows buffalo retreating from an eroded landscape in Southern Rhodesia. The land is dead.

The most terrible and virtually uncontrollable agent against wild animals is drought. When animals starve it means that either there are too many (which seldom comes about) or that domestic herds have stripped the land (which happens with depressing frequency). The partly-starved antelopes *above* drinking at a mudhole are victims of man-made desolation.

Right: This elephant in the Naso-Nyvio River in Kenya, had been stricken with anthrax. Even the vultures would not eat it.

Chapter 25

LOST TO THE WORLD

"WILL history books say that Twentieth-Century Man was too preoccupied with reaching for the Moon to bother about saving one of the richest and most precious inheritances on his earth?"—*Daily Mirror* on wild life.

The cheetah, one of the swiftest animals in the world—one kept up with our estate car at 40 m.p.h.—makes a lithe, graceful and affectionate pet. Its existence is in grave jeopardy.

The gorilla has a spine-chilling majesty and strength of frame which has given him a regal place among the forest beasts. It is high on the death list.

The huge forms of rhino, white and black, are fading before our eyes like the Cheshire cat in *Alice in Wonderland* Can they be reprieved?

Many other species are also seriously threatened, for every day wild animals are suffering grisly, frequently long-drawn-out and pitifully painful deaths; and man in the mass is indifferent to this modern tragedy. Over 100 types of animals have vanished from the earth. Hundreds more species may be under sentence of death.

"The enemies of game are the men who grudge it living room, grazing and water; who fear its depredations and who covet its trophies regardless of cost," says Chief A. S. Fundikira of Tanganyika. "We must provide for all of them. But, above all, we must work out ways of convincing the man who imagines himself to be immediately threatened by game that it is to his ultimate advantage to keep that game."

The Director-General of Unesco has strongly supported this view by stating that although man may be considered the most fully evolved of living creatures he is none the less the most destructive. By this reckless exploitation of the natural wealth for short-sighted economic purposes, man had upset the delicate biological balance of Nature and was thus responsible for the extinction of many animal species. His passion for destruction had been the cause of many famines. Even the last sanctuaries of wild life, the national parks, were themselves threatened.

The main factors which have contributed, and are contributing, to the destruction of game and their habitats, chiefly at the hands of man, are:

1. Lack of water conservation to ensure the survival of animals in seasonal droughts, and an equal lack of anti-erosion measures in the subsequent floods.
2. African population explosions.
3. Organized poaching by both old and new methods.
4. The officially-organized wholesale killings of game herds in efforts to stamp out diseases of humans and livestock transmitted by the tsetse fly.
5. The invasion and cutting down of forests for timber and firewood.
6. Agricultural development, and the over-grazing by cattle in large numbers.
7. Illicit hunting on a wide scale by Europeans and others.
8. Bush fires (always a terrifying sight to man and animal) which have been deliberately started for one or other of the following reasons: to clear the bush and forest and to provide fresh grazing of tender grass shoots from charred stubble; by poachers to drive the animals towards the guns, spears and snares; as part of tsetse fly control operations.

All these subjects, coupled with heartfelt pleas for money, and more money, came up time and time again in speeches and papers delivered by delegates to the Arusha conference.

As I have shown in two particularly harrowing instances, during the drought periods in Africa many rivers dry up and those that keep running are in some cases so far away from what sparse grazing is left that animals must choose whether to die of starvation or thirst. In August, 1961, it was reported that already 25 per cent of the 40,000 head of game in the Nairobi Royal National Park had died.

Those skeletons which the delegates to the Arusha conference saw on each side of the road on their journey from Nairobi were of animals which were the victims of circumstance, retreating before advancing civilization in the form of human settlements, robbed of pastures by domestic herds of cattle, hard hit by drought and their reproductive potential retarded. They had wandered frantically through man-made deserts created by over-grazing and, like others elsewhere, fell an easy prey to poachers and to disease when exhaustion overtook them. Fleeing or hemmed in, hundreds of thousands of animals from tiny dikdiks to fully-grown elephants are dying like this in Africa. Her human population (as a result of the white man's medicines, science and husbandry and an end to most tribal wars followed by the take-over of marginal lands) doubles itself in well under every forty years, whereas the game survival graph plunges steeply downward.

Animals in most West African countries, for instance, have been crowded out by the teeming and rapidly-increasing African populations, and wild animals in any number and variety can be seen today only around the shores of Lake Chad.

"Penicillin has wrecked the balance of Nature," Dr. Verschuren complained to me in the Congo. "It is a curse."

War, too, had taken its toll in another region of Dr. Verschuren's adopted country. Despite pressure from several quarters on the United Nations to ensure the survival of the national parks in the former Belgian Congo until the country's internecine strife was over, nothing had been done in this respect by the world organization by the end of 1961. The biggest of the Nature sanctuaries in the Congo, the Upemba National Park, set in the heart of mineral-rich Katanga, was a tragic contrast to the Parc Albert in Kivu. A handbook on Upemba printed shortly before independence provided a touch of sad irony in describing the Park as constituting "a precious collection of Nature reserves which elsewhere vanish under the impact of disruption and destruction."

Upemba, situated among landscapes and wooded valleys of typical Katanga forestland, once sheltered a rich selection of the larger mammal fauna such as elephant and buffalo as well as large zebra herds which lived together with eland and black and roan antelopes. Even then the few black rhino in the region were struggling for survival, and now they may well have gone forever. For Upemba was a shambles at the time I visited Katanga; it had become a battleground of Katangese soldiers in their Belgian-type jungle-camouflage uniforms and their enemies, the fierce and fanatical cannibals of the Baluba tribe.

The Belgian warden of the Park had stayed on after independence but, in the face of internal strife and without funds from the coffers of the Tshombe Goverment, gave up in mid-1961 and returned to Europe, leaving behind his home in the Park and the crumbling chalets of the tourist camp.

In Elisabethville I sought permission from various black ministers and officials to visit Upemba. My applications were summarily rejected. I was told that the Balubas of the area, who fight with poisoned arrows and crude muzzle-loaders filled with soft-lead shot and nails, had vowed to kill all whites and were constantly on murderous rampages. "You would never leave the Park alive, Monsieur," said a clerk in one of the Ministries.

A Polish mercenary friend who had been on active service with the Katangese forces in Upemba a few weeks before told me that all the African game rangers and guides there had fled, adding: "Anyone can shoot there now as much as he likes, but it would be a highly-dangerous business, not on account of the animals but because man himself has turned the Park into a cockpit of war." He said that both the Katangese soldiers, using sub-machine guns and other automatic weapons, and the Balubas themselves were indiscriminately shooting out the animals for food, and there were great fears for the elephant population which was believed to include a monster with tusks of 180 lb. each.

A white hunter who now works as a civil servant in Elisabethville told me that, despite its wealth, the Katanga Government had done nothing to save the Park. "Here the copper mines and the railways work and that's all that matters," he said.

In the Albertville district of Northern Katanga, Balubas, he claimed, had killed 1,500 elephant for ivory and food over a matter of months, and there had been a great deal of rhino killing throughout Katanga in the past, on the orders of the chiefs themselves, to obtain horns to sell to Asians.

"The less security in Africa, the less game," sighed the ex-white hunter.

One elephant in chaotic Katanga seems assured of a long life. This particular specimen inhabits the southern part, has four tusks, and the tribesmen believe this rare creature contains the soul of a Paramount Chief. Accorded the status of a god, the animal browses in complete safety.

Soldiers and provincial policemen in Ethiopia, far from being guardians of the scrappy and ill-applied game laws, are said to be the principal offenders in illicit killings, sometimes to the extent of wantonly mowing down groups of animals with machine-guns more for "sport" than meat, or, like the cruellest of professional poachers, only for comercially-valuable trophies.

The Serengeti poaching story I have told can, as you read this chapter, be multiplied a hundred times or more all over Africa.

Professor Huxley says the abolition of this "shocking" trade is becoming just as compelling an aim as was the abolition of the slave trade in Africa a century ago. Anyone who has seen a baby elephant squealing in anguish beside a 12-ft.-deep pit in which its mother has died a lingering death, or the heaving, bloody pile of a three-legged giraffe which has torn itself away from the deep-biting, devilish noose of a steel-wire snare into which it had stumbled would share his anger and revulsion. I have met European game wardens who, if the law allowed (and they feel it an injustice that it does not) would willingly chop off the right hand of any ivory or rhino-horn poacher they or their rangers catch. Such men and their colleagues have no time either for those who would defend the meat poacher for "supplying a national demand", or for people in authority, European or African, who condone poaching or advocate treating poachers lightly either on account of misplaced paternalism or through a desire to catch election votes.

National parks and reserves where game abound are the main targets of poachers. In both Northern and Southern Rhodesia poachers, when discovered, have savagely attacked African game guards. The poachers use packs of dogs, spears and shotguns. Four game guards have been brutally murdered by poachers in the remote Luangwa Valley game reserve in Northern Rhodesia, and in a national park near Fort Victoria, Southern Rhodesia, another gang clubbed a park policeman to death with knobkerries.

Poachers in the 5,000-square-mile Wankie National Park in Southern Rhodesia near the Victoria Falls—the Park abounds with elephant families—are extremely mobile Bushmen who work in bands of up to a dozen men, women and children. They are well equipped with weapons, snares and pack donkeys. There are also white poachers in the Park.

A paper prepared by Thane Riney and Mr. B. Austen of the Park states: "The poacher accepts the risks involved and when caught will often take the consequences and refuse to give the name of his "sponsor", either from loyalty, or fear of reprisals to himself or his family. . . . Poaching no longer occurs on a large scale while the mobility of the ranger force ensures that a poacher cannot establish himself in an area for any length of time or is able to operate in a team on a large scale."

Because, however, the nature of the Wankie Park often precludes the use of motor vehicles, the anti-poaching measures there consist of a series of two-man foot patrols following different routes each month.

Large areas of the Kafue Park in Northern Rhodesia have been laid waste by fires started by poachers.

"Poaching is Big Business," says Peter L. Achard, a Serengeti game ranger. "The poachers are making easy money, and, if they are caught, they merely pay their fines, or they are paid for them, and go straight back to poaching. They soon recover what little they have lost."

There is no mechanism in the most primitive form of wild animal trap used by some African poachers and hunters. The unsuspecting animal walks into a prepared and disguised cavity such as a pitfall. The ordinary "game pit" is common to a number of countries in Africa, but the humane efforts of wild-life societies have helped to make the barbarous pit with sharpened stakes almost a snare of the past. In rural African communities, however, a modified form still survives although, as one warden put it to me, "Thank God, most of the beggars are too lazy to dig."

Also used by Africans are the simple, inhuman "falling log" and "falling stone" traps. The "falling log" is usually placed at intervals round the village cropland or gardens, in the fence or on paths leading to water. The victim, in attempting to squeeze through the opening, releases the log and is pinned down. It may be days before the animal is dragged out and killed.

The "falling stone" is supported by one end of a stick which rests on a forked stick carrying a string holding a trigger. The mechanism is so arranged that seeds placed below the rock attract rodents and birds which release the triger and are entombed.

The "Muneba", made of strong grass which grows near river banks, is a conical, tapered trap used for catching field-or cane-rats which, stewed, make a tasty meal. The men and youths leave their huts in the early morning and place the traps at strategic points on paths or runs. The long grass around is then beaten, and the rats driven into the traps where they are clubbed to death as they huddle together.

Many Africans in Rhodesia regard the days of "good hunting" as a thing of the past. In early times when elephants were hunted without guns, it was believed no elephant could resist a certain sweet-smelling *muti* or medicine. The medicine was sprinkled on the ground, and the hunters went into hiding. The tribe's swiftest runner, attired in white skins, would go out in search of a herd.

He would dance and prance before the elephants, leading them to where they could smell the scent of the *muti*. When the animals commenced to dig the ground with their tusks, the hunters would emerge and set upon them with assegais and arrows. Tribal stories have it that at all times throughout the attacks the elephants would be addressed in terms of glowing respect. When an elephant was finally overpowered, a selected hero or *mhari* would step forward with an axe and proceed to hamstring the wounded animal. The elephant would generally fall on the side of his digging tusk. As it fell on the land, the tusk was regarded as the property of the chief and was carried to him.

A game scout who notched on his arms the number of elephants he killed on game control and crop protection duties, has just retired from the Tanganyika Game Division. Mr. M. Ndaiga, of Matongoro who has always claimed that a piece of elephant brain rubbed into an incision in either arm was a foolproof method of self-preservation. He reckoned that by possessing elephant brains he was able to think like an elephant and so anticipate any move by the elephant he was hunting.

"Judging by the numerous scars on his arms it would appear this practice has stood him in good stead," said his game warden.

Another custom observed in the bush has been the hunting of eland in pairs. It was considered unlucky for an African hunter to be seen by the dying animal after he had shot it, so the attacker would remain concealed while his companion finished off the eland.

* * *

A tough African insect, the tsetse fly, which is smaller than a child's fingernail, has been responsible for the deaths of massive numbers of game animals. But the white man has as gruesome a record as the actual murderer, with the little tsetse fly merely an accessory before the fact.

For all that, there is nothing endearing about this swift, silent blood-sucking fly with its characteristic crossed scissor-blade wings. Carrying sleeping sickness, once one of Africa's great scourges, and the deadly *nagana* disease of cattle, transmitting the parasites to wild animals (which, being acclimatized, are rarely affected) the fly is a menace to both domestic livestock and to human beings, though now to a very much smaller degree than at the turn of the century. It needs shade for breeding.

With a quarter of the entire continent infested with tsetse fly, several countries in Africa have grim histories of ruthless game slaughters in sustained but mainly abortive campaigns to eradicate the fly. Where a measure of success was attained, usually it was only temporary, because small species, such as rodents, generally escape the slaughter and continue to act as vectors. Investigations, quoted by Grizmek, into the origin of the blood sucked by tsetse flies in East Africa indicated that warthogs and bush pigs furnished most of the blood while buffaloes accounted for about 5 per cent. Roan antelopes, kudu and bushbuck between them yielded another 15 per cent. Domestic cattle, sheep and goats also were bitten regularly. The most common grazing animals were not bitten at all and the tsetse flies rarely attacked the eland, duiker, waterbuck, impala, baboon, monkey, dogs, cats and hyenas.

In Zululand in 1942 *nagana* took hold, and a widespread destruction of all wild animals was instituted. In eight years 138,329 head of game were shot, but the disease was not put down.

A recent annual report of the Southern Rhodesian Government's Department of Wild Life Conservation records that areas of hunting in the Colony under tsetse fly control were still further restricted, and that there had been a decrease in the number of animals shot—17,961 in 1960 as compared to 18,583 in the previous year. The report adds: "Much more intensive work is being done in the development of insecticides and bush clearing as a means of tsetse control."

Southern Rhodesia has a black record in the eyes of the world for the destruction of game to kill tsetse flies in settlement areas. by depriving the flies of their food supply.

Up to 1945, 326,469 animals, including lion, rhino, elephant, buffalo, kudu, zebra, duiker and other species, had been destroyed to put down tsetse fly in the colony, and in the following ten years there was an average annual massacre of between 20,000 and 30,000 animals a year. Hundreds of African hunters, under the supervision of European tsetse rangers, worked in pairs over ten-square-mile areas armed with rifles and ball ammunition. As the Commission of Inquiry on Human and Animal Trypanoso-miasis in Southern Rhodesia was told in 1955, many of the African hunters did not shoot well enough and animals escaped to die, or live on, in agony; the system of allowing the hunters to sell or barter the meat and hides led to selective shooting as apart from general game elimination (the hunters obtained tails from outside their areas to hand over to the tsetse ranger, and so give the impression that more game had been killed in their area than was the fact).

The Commission was told that game destruction had been the principal measure for the control of the tsetse fly in Southern Rhodesia *because it was the most economical method over large areas.* The Commission urged that the Trypanosomiasis Committee, "whose name has become associated in the public mind with the slaughter of game," should be reconstituted and renamed. The report continued: "Having reviewed the various methods of control in use in various parts of Africa, and those suggested by various witnesses, we conclude that the only ones we can recommend for serious consideration and investigation as to application to the territory's problems are discriminative clearing, combined with close settlement, and, in special circumstances, the use of modern insecticides; but it must be clearly stated that until the proper methods of application of these new measures have been worked out, it will be necessary to continue modified game destruction under more strict control."

During the year that the Commission sat 41,886 game animals were destroyed in Southern Rhodesia's tsetse fly control areas and in the following year 34,207. But in 1957 the Commission's recommendations took a marked effect. Only 18,000 animals were slaughtered.

The end of thirty years of the wholesale killing system, an end which had been made possible through the development of effective insecticides and cattle drugs, was reported two years ago by Mr. J. Ford, Director of the Colony's Tsetse and Trypanoso-miasis Control and Reclamation. Ground spraying, he said, had proved more effective than shooting following experiments in the use of knapsack insecticide sprayers operated by Africans in a heavily-infested area of 100-square-miles. Only those parts of the bush essential to the fly's life were sprayed, about five per cent of the total area. Yet within one week of spraying the incidence of fly dropped by from 75 to 80 per cent.

On every occasion that I went out in the Land-Rover during my visits to Serengeti, little clouds of tsetse swarmed into the vehicle and, picturing myself lying mortally ill after a single bite, I exhausted myself wielding a rolled-up newspaper to beat off these sinister and persistent intruders. Nothing but a forcibly delivered direct hit deterred them. Idly rolling a fly between his thumb and forefinger and ignoring those which had settled on his legs, neck and arms, the warden guide remarked: "Take it easy. These chaps are the real guardians of the Park, you know. Without them those lions over there—and all the other animals —would sooner or later have to give way to the land-hungry and the cattle."

Uganda is one big country in Africa which still has much to learn, and that at a time when the activities of some white officials arouse a dangerous cynicism in the black inhabitants. In a recent anti-tsetse game-killing campaign in the Ankole district of the country some 28,000 wild animals were exterminated in just over two years. Of these there were 8,500 bushbuck, 7,000 duiker, 4,000 reedbuck and 2,500 waterbuck. No meat or hides were utilized. The campaign had a "deplorable" effect on public opinion, meaning the African masses who saw this slaughter at a time when they were being counselled to protect wild life.

"If only the die-hard Tsetse Control Department can be prevented from continuing its extermination campaign in the mistaken impression that it is permanently clearing the fly-infested areas, long after other territories have abandoned this out-dated policy," declared angry Game Department officials who attended a conference at Entebbe early in 1962, "Uganda should have a flourishing wild life industry which will be a unique, and highly profitable, national and economic asset."

Chapter 26

ACTIONS AND INTENTIONS

THERE is a housing shortage—for lions—in Nairobi, but they like to take evening strolls through the suburbs. The 1962 annual report of the Kenya Royal National Parks records that lion families from Nairobi's Game Park are regularly seen plodding through gardens and between houses in fashionable Langata where a number of hunters, both active and retired, have their homes. The residents invite friends round for "sundowners" and sit on their verandas to watch the lions go by!

"It is always astonishing why lions, which normally love it in the Park, find reason to wander out of it," writes the Park Warden, Stephen Ellis. "In their own sanctuary they have all they require to eat, and enough water to drink."

He believes that the itinerant lions may be bored with their usual surroundings.

The Nairobi lions, according to the same annual report, have developed a taste for chewing up plastic hose-pipe in the park, but whether or not this is as a result of their nightly excursions through the city's suburbia is not stated.

Long before tamed lions became the subjects of best-selling books, Mr. Ellis reared from a cub a male lion which played like a cat on the lawn of his home, and loved to hide behind bushes at the entrance to the house to pounce out on African callers and push them off their bicycles. The family's lion was presented to the Queen, then Princess Elizabeth, when she visited the Nairobi Royal National Park. Given the name of "Prince", he was later shipped to a zoo in England.

Lions in general are the most inquisitive of animals, and will not rest until their abounding curiosity is satisfied. There is the story, still to be confirmed, of the party of tourists with a battery-transistor portable television set under a baobab at dusk in a remote part of Southern Rhodesia who glanced round to find a lion crouched in the grass intently following an American cowboy film.

Time and time again, greenhorn travellers in the bush have found to their cost that to erect thorn and branch fences round their camps at night has served to attract, rather than keep away, lions which come from afar to examine these strange structures that are out of harmony with their day-to-day surroundings. They are liable to attack in panic if disturbed in their nocturnal investigations.

Apart from the odd man-eater and at mating and cubbing seasons, lions are not usually aggressive towards humans although in the past they have been regarded by the majority of Africans as vermin to be tracked down and killed off for war-dress trophies. Lion manes made headdresses for Masai warriors who, aspiring to the coveted title of "Lion Killer", had first to seize the cornered beast by the tail before—drugged with potions of secret herbs— plunging home spears single-handed.

Now strictly preserved, lions take a heavy toll of antelope and zebra without the herds being seriously affected by this natural culling, but, if these are scarce and hunger demands, they will tackle larger animals like hippo and buffalo in hard, yet not always successful, fights. In Uganda one lion was found to have had its shoulder torn off in fatal combat with a hippo which it had marked down for a banquet.

Last year, visitors to the Wankie Game Reserve in Southern Rhodesia, watching tensely from their cars, witnessed a gladiatorial drama when a pride of nine lions ambushed a sable antelope in a shallow, treeless gulley. Lion after lion attacked the trapped animal. Each time the lions were driven back by wide sweeps of the sable's needle-sharp horns.

"None of us gave much for the poor thing's chances against overwhelming odds," said Mr. Ron Blackmore, a Rhodesian amateur photographer who took blow-by-blow shots of the incident. "One by one the lions went in to try to drag the animal down. After being roundly repulsed, each one thought better of it. Those horns could have slashed them open like a sword. Finally, the sable turned his back on the last of the attackers, a large lioness, and stalked off."

A burst of cheering and clapping from the onlookers saluted the sable's brave victory.

"Perhaps the applause was the last indignity," says Mr. Blackmore. "With a roar, the lioness gave chase. But by this time the sable was well clear and showed her a clean pair of heels."

A lion kill is popularly considered to be a swift and merciful business, but the only one I have seen—in southern Tanganyika—was gruesome and prolonged. While the male yawned in the shade of an acacia, three of five lionesses loped off towards a group of grazing zebra while the other two remained behind tufts of long grass. Surrounding the zebra, the "beaters" edged in on their bellies and drove them towards their hidden companions.

A low grunt was followed by a tawny flash. As the rest of the herd scattered in all directions with eyes rolling, a zebra stallion staggered and stumbled as a lioness clawed bloody streaks in its hindquarters. A second lioness sprang and caught the zebras neck tightly in her jaws. The stricken, frantically-struggling stallion sank down under the weight of its assailants. For ten minutes or more the zebra twitched and kicked spasmodically as the lionesses, now joined by the other three, leisurely tore open its stomach and throat and began their meal, pausing now and then to look around, while it was still dying.

When, at last, the zebra lay still and the haunches were being ripped apart, the male lion ambled over from his vantage point and, disdainfully shouldering aside the females, settled down by the carcass and began gnawing a set of ribs.

As a rule, lions live, mate and hunt together amicably in large prides. Lionesses appear to be willing to mate with several males in the pride in the course of a few days.

Man-eaters prowl alone with infinite cunning.

It was in Tanganyika that an old black-maned lion, having mauled and devoured an African child, took to raiding villages and carrying off men and women. For months the tribespeople lived in terror as the lion defied all attempts by spearmen to wound or kill it. The headman of each of the villages visited by the lion sacrificed a cow, and a witchdoctor, wearing a snarling wooden mask and black ostrich plumes, was called in.

Squatting down, he muttered incantations, cast strange spells and flung baboon bones and strips of lion skin in the dust before flourishing a beer bottle at the gaping crowd around him. Sealing the neck with grey mud, he announced gravely that the man-eater was safely inside the bottle and would trouble the villages no more. He ordered the bottle to be buried four feet deep under a rock.

The raids ceased from that hour: the man-killer was never seen again. Had it died a violent or natural death on its grim wanderings, making the witchdoctor's "magic" just a coincidence? Africa always offers a fascinating choice of solutions to such mysteries.

There is now evidence which may support theories that there is some form of telepathy between the lions and tribalized Africans who have been known to use the kingly beasts to hunt buck and share their prey with them. The Fauna Preservation Society meeting in London in May, 1962, was told that one of these "lion controllers" (in Tanganyika) had been sent to prison by a local chief after villagers had protested against killings by lions. The chief, it was stated, was warned by the gaoled man that unless he was freed by nightfall he would "tell" his lions to kill the chief's cattle.

The chief refused.

Next morning fourteen of his cows, severely mauled, lay dead.

*   *   *

During my last visit to the city of Nairobi, a pampered, amiable and talented African lion—"It can do everything but read the script," said the director—was brought to the entrance of my hotel in a large car as a publicity stunt. It had travelled in almost-human luxury from Hollywood to star in a film being made near Nanyuki.

Hundreds of urban African workers, grinning, shouting and gesticulating in wonder, thronged the street outside the hotel and, boisterously pushing aside steel-helmeted riot police, jostled the bored and listless animal. There were excited cries of "Simba!" This was a thrill that they, deep in Africa, had forgotten and their eyes glowed and rolled at the sight again of one of the noble creatures woven into memories of their childhood and past tribal glories.

There was a symbolism and a nagging moral in that scene.

How can the animals be saved? With only 10 per cent left of the game's once staggering numbers, these, I feel, are now the only key factors for survival:

1. National parks.
2. Game ranching and game farming.
3. Development of ecology.
4. Cash.

If more than a few relics are to be preserved for scientific studies and the enjoyment of future generations, it seems likely that all parks will have to be fenced except on migration routes. Fencing, admittedly a highly-costly business, might also act as a brake on the sanctioned "shrinkage" of parks under political pressures.

As I write this there lies on my desk a statement by Sir Malcom Barrow, the Deputy Prime Minister, announcing that two-thirds of the unfenced Matopos National Park near Bulawayo,

The photograph *above* was taken in the Wankie Game Reserve. A pride of nine lions had ambushed a sable antelope. but none dared to come within the sweep of the great curved horns. The incident and its outcome are described on page 206.

Below: Enlarged from a single frame on a small cinematograph film, this picture shows sable bulls fighting. Such incidents are comparatively rare, but the possibility of being able to record something of this kind is one of the great incentives to the taking of a camera into Africa's sanctuaries where wild animals live free.

Above: Two kinds of fisherman, men and birds, working together in harmony. The fishermen are netting Lake Edward near Ishasha in Uganda for Tilapia, a highly edible fish. The marabou storks wander among the returning boats and promptly devour the offal from gutted fish. This is an example of symbiosis, or mutual dependence. Can man come to terms also with others of Africa's wild animals?

Mount Kenya used to be covered with a superb forest of cedars. They were cut down to make casual work for unemployed Kikuyu who wanted small patches of cultivatable ground. The cedars were replaced by imported pine trees which were promptly attacked by a local bark-boring beetle. Soon there will be no vegetation on this slope of the mountain above Nanyuki.

150,000 acres, have been excised and handed over to 650 African families. Only 90,000 acres of the area, close to the grave of Cecil John Rhodes, the founder of Rhodesia, have been left as a park, but these do include all the main tourist routes and amenities; the headwaters, watercourses, streams and dams. Before the hand-over, the tribesmen living on the parkland claimed that Rhodes had given it to them. They threatened members of the Park's staff whose work conflicted with their agricultural activities. Game animals were snared and others killed not only for meat but as wanton gestures of defiance.

"The welfare of the African families settled within the area has always been a major consideration, and the various authorities concerned came to the conclusion that the only proper use—in the interests of the State and the people as a whole—would be to allow those families to remain," declared Sir Malcolm after his Government's capitulation.

★   ★   ★

ASPECTS TO LAND HUNGER

Land hunger among Africans, linked to increasing population pressures and industrial and other development, is a major factor to be taken into account in the battle to save the game and natural resources. It is one which must become of increasing importance. There are, nevertheless, still huge areas of land in several African countries—for example, the former Belgian Congo and Portuguese African territories—available for basic occupation.

In countries which have not yet attained African governments the plea of "land hunger" is often a political parrot-cry in the struggle for freedom and, on close examination, may be found to be more theoretical than practical.

Kenya, which has many tied acres purchased in the early days, has acute land problems. The population pressure in Tanganyika, however, is not the same as in Southern Rhodesia where the Native birth rate has nearly doubled itself over the last twenty years.

In the Colony Africans can no longer get land, virtually free, from the chiefs. It has to be bought and sold on a controlled, competitive basis.

Throughout Africa the indigenous people range from naked tribesmen living under bare subsistence conditions to a whole range of prosperous businessmen and well-educated professional men such as barristers, university lecturers, clergymen, doctors, journalists, company secretaries, headmasters and school-teachers, police officers, trade union organizers, and civil servants.

The proportion of Africa's black numbers who are sophisticated by Western standards is still not noticeably high, but it is growing month by month and year by year with the extension of educational facilities, the development of economic opportunities and the provision of financial aid grants.

Between these two poles, the African peoples are at all stages of development although the majority still live pastoral or agricultural lives in their tribal areas. But more and more of the younger generation are gravitating towards the cities and towns and looking back to the land as a means of subsistence only if they cannot find employment in these centres.

It may be to the ultimate advantage of the game that manages to survive that there is a growing class of African which seeks a permanent livelihood in urban areas, working in government departments, and in all branches of industry and commerce.

TOURISM

Many more tourists must be attracted to the parks throughout Africa to provide the finance for additional facilities and increased staff and equipment, including light aircraft or small helicopters to fight the poachers.

As an African speaker put it to the conference at Arusha, for centuries the wild life of Africa has stirred the imagination of men in other lands with its promise of adventure. "Nowhere else in the world can one see such an abundance and variety of animals in their natural setting. In addition, we have a good climate, beautiful scenery, snow-capped mountains, the attractions of the coast and many picturesque scenes of African life. But these are all secondary in drawing power to the wild animals—it is the lion, the elephant, the rhino, and the herds of other game which together form the primary attraction. It is these that we can set against the cathedrals and art galleries of other countries as our own contribution to the cultural heritage of mankind."

And how much stronger today for millions more people in the feverish, modern Western world is Africa's promise of adventure, or the lure of an escape from the constantly-threatened horrors of nuclear warfare, domestic claustrophobia, mechanization and regimentation to seek the balm of the raw primeval?

Professor Huxley expressed the view in his 1960 report to Unesco that most tribal Africans regarded wild animals either as a pest to be destroyed or simply as meat on the hoof to be killed and eaten. He underlined this by pointing out that in several African languages there was the same word for both "meat" and "wild animals". He found then that educated and politically-minded Africans tended to have rather different attitudes. Some of them regarded national parks and controlled shooting areas as relics of white "colonialism", or merely as places where white men could indulge their peculiar habit of enjoying the sight or the pursuit of wild animals. On that account these Africans regard the parks as things to be abolished, or at any rate not encouraged. Professor Huxley added: "Others retort in ways like this: 'You white men have killed all your wolves and bears: Why do you want us Africans to preserve our lions and elephants?' This type of argument often accompanies a more deep-seated attitude—the feeling that emergent Africa must at all costs become "modern' and that large wild animals in a country are the reverse of modern, and, indeed, a badge of primitivism."

In two years, however, it seemed the African *élite* had been convinced of the exact opposite (and one can imagine the patient, persistent lobbying by European experts involved) for, after Arusha, Professor Huxley wrote this heartening tribute: "It is often asserted that Africans have no feeling for Nature or beauty, and think of wild animals only as a source of meat. This is not true. The conference drove home the fact that wild life and Nature can be a source of pride and prestige, both national and tribal, and local. I would prophesy that emergent nations of Africa will soon set about establishing national parks, if only because to be without any will stigmatize them as uncivilized." Several others prominent in the field of game conservation, like Dr. Verschuren, have a similar comforting and encouraging outlook.

MAINTAINING A BALANCE OF NATURE

Europeans in Kenya and elsewhere who farm near those national parks where, as yet, no controlled cropping of game animals has been instituted, are sharply critical of those in control and indignant at the continued delay in the implementation of what they, supported by a growing number of conservationists, regard as a fundamental necessity. "A dustbowl is creeping at a pretty fast gallop from the Serengeti right up to the doorstep of Nairobi, a dustbowl whose magnitude would make the Colorado dustbowl look like a child's sandpit in comparison," writes a white farmer in the Nairobi district in a letter to the *East African Standard*.

"In order to maintain a normal balance of Nature on one's farm, stock to grass, normal prudence demands that one should cull at least 50 per cent of one's herd annually. If one does not obey this simple rule of Nature, the results are disastrous; one's farm becomes a desert and the cattle die or else break out and start trespassing all around the district in search of food. Yet within the game parks we have the absurd picture of two stiff-necked bodies, on the one side the Masai, their pride forbidding them to cull out their cattle, and, on the other, the game parks with their, to put it mildly, wishy-washy policy of no destocking. Between them they are making an absolute shambles, not only of the land with which they have been entrusted but also of the vast surrounding area of farming lands.

"We are sitting on what should be the loveliest and wealthiest stock farm in the world. Why, in a land of plenty, can I not buy a haunch of venison from the butcher?"

Europeans in charge must point the way to their eventual African successors by inaugurating organized game-cropping in the parks and reserves together with arranging the subsequent transport, storage and economic marketing of regulated amounts of venison, biltong and trophies from (as applicable where the habitats are threatened owing to an excess of numbers) such animals as the heavy-yielding elephant, hippo and buffalo, and zebra, wildebeest and antelope.

NATIVE CUSTOMS AND SUPERSTITIONS

Some African customs and practices hinder game preservation. One very important cause of trouble is over-grazing. The problem is overall in Africa with hundreds of tribes, whose wealth is counted not in cash but in cattle, constantly moving their herds from place to place to find and demolish the best grazing. The moving herds leave behind large areas denuded of all vegetation but inedible weeds and ripe for soil erosion by the wind. The Nilo-Hamitic Masai provide the most blatant example of this practice, although in certain areas some are beginning to settle down.

Camels, which are still the chief form of their "bride wealth" (tribesmen in other parts of Africa generally use cattle for *lobola*, the purchase of wives), are the mainstay of the Rendille who inhabit Kenya's arid Northern Province where the lava rock and scrub patches support less than one person to every square mile. The camels are slaughtered for meat, but also provide the tribe with milk and transport. These skin-clad people now have an almost equal number of cattle, sheep and goats and the continual search for water and grazing for these animals is made at the cost of the few species of wild game living in the area.

Ruthless hunters in East Africa are the 80,000-strong Turkana who are found up to the Ethiopian border and are linked with tribes in the Sudan and Uganda. Apparently possessing iron stomachs, they have the reputation of being able to eat and enjoy any of the wild things they kill so freely, be it a snake or a three-foot lizard.

Fellow destroyers of game on a pitiless scale are the Boran, who belong to the Galla group, original invaders of Uganda and Kenya from Ethiopia. The Boran still roam over a wide section of the Northern Province in Kenya, but there are concentrations around Marsabit, Garba Tulla and Moyale where, using camels and ponies over harsh ground, they strike down wild life in the largest possible numbers with spears and a variety of other tribal weapons. Cattle represent their fortunes.

The Waliangulu, a hardy group of elephant hunters who live in the coarse, coast hinterland bordering on Tsavo Royal National Park, are, like the Boni, Asi and Sanye to whom they are related, expert marksmen with the bow and arrow, using powerful poisons to kill the grey giants and other big game. On the slim credit side, they have in some cases assisted in the tracking down and killing of elephant in official culling operations.

The stunted, forest-dwelling Dorobo, of whom these are now only about 100 pure families in Kenya, are believed to share a common origin with the Bushmen and, like them, live by hunting. A Masai legend says that at the beginning of the world a Dorobo gave birth to a boy and a girl, who issued from his shin bone, and they became the ancestors of the whole human race.

There are a few bright passages in our tale of the relations between Africa's tribesmen and the animals.

For instance, the Kipsigis, the most southerly of the Kalenjin-speaking peoples of Kenya, once lived like the Masai and laid waste the land with their large herds of cattle. Under the guidance of European officials of the British administration, however, the Kipsigis settled down and have since made rapid progress in agriculture. Their reserve is a model African farming area, well fenced, paddocked and sustaining an increasing number of good-quality cattle.

Although the youths still instinctively spear big game behind the backs of the elders, the Samburu tribesmen of Northern Kenya, who proudly call themselves "the world's top people", have also adopted government measures in animal husbandry and are today hailed as "in the forefront of Africa's nomadic cattle people". The 35,000 members of the Samburu, also Nilo-Hamites, own 350,000 hump-backed cattle which, despite being grazed on scorched plains, produce good beef. Jealously, the Masai have nicknamed the Samburu "butterflies".

In the south and some other parts of Africa superstition helps to spare some types of wild animals.

An acquaintance of mine, then an officer in the British South Africa Police, was on a horse patrol in the Sabi Valley of Southern Rhodesia with an African detective, an educated and intelligent man, and shot a young eland for the pot. As the animal sank to the ground with a bullet in its heart, the African let out a howl of anguish. In tears, he explained that the spirit of the founder of his branch of a tribe lived on in the eland—other tribesmen believe that the leopard, zebra, waterbuck or some other creature or wild bird contains the spirit forms of their chiefs—and, consequently, he and his fellows had been given the native name for the animal, their "brother", and was forbidden to kill or injure it. That African policeman was ravenously hungry after being all day on the trail without food, but he refused to touch a morsel of the eland shoulder which was roasted over the camp fire.

ECONOMICS AND PUBLICITY

One question asked is, "How can you convince Africans in general that killing animals in the parks is wrong when you are selling game-meat from those parks to them?" The managing and cropping on a broad scale of wild life within Africa's parks would have to be allied to propaganda campaigns designed to convince Africans at all stages of development that in this way better, cheaper and more meat is provided than by poachers, and that the well-being of the animals and vegetation alike, meaning guaranteed and probably bigger profits, would be improved. Humane, sentimental or scientific reasons make little impact.

Both inside and outside the parks, a wide variety of wild animals can yield a high crop of protein from the land where, with cropping where designed or necessary, they ensure full cycles of fertility through eating the vegetation, according to species, below, on and above the ground.

In parts of South Africa people are advertising for game to put on their farms. Why shoot out the animals and then spend small fortunes trying to replace them?

Thane Riney, excited and deeply impressed after a tour of the Transvaal, said that over the last five years the number of farms there stocking game had averaged between 2,000 and 3,000.

"The cost of running game is negligible," he added. "No special feeding or dipping is needed. Any extra fencing required is soon paid for out of profits from the sale of meat. On some farms, the only cost is bullets for the annual harvesting. Buck and antelope are being run with cattle, or on the same ranch but separate from the cattle, sometimes with rotation of grazing areas. I have seen a combination of blesbok and mealie-growing. It worked. The variety of economically-productive pieces of game that any one farm can stock depends on the country and vegetation, but I saw two farms with between twelve and fifteen species on them. Five species is common. The species, suitably combined for the kind of country, do not encroach on each others diets. In some of the dry *lowveld* country, the game is actually helping to maintain or build up the land which before was on the downgrade. This is one of its most important benefits."

From personal knowledge, I am able to record with admiration the extensive and very valuable work which has been done, and is being done, in the field of applied ecology or, in other words, conservation of natural resources and game by individual American and British experts, a number of whom have made considerable financial sacrifices to undertake their research.

In January, 1962, the New York Zoological Society opened a

campaign to raise $7,000,000 for a number of projects, including wild-life protection in Africa. In the previous year the Society contributed $39,000 to be used in training Africans in wild-life management and other conservation measures. Fairfield Osborn, President of the Society which runs the Bronx Zoo and the Aquarium in Brooklyn, announced that scientific research and education would be considerably expanded during 1962.

At about the same time an Englishman and an American started an extensive tour of Africa to investigate the wild life situation for the United Nations Food and Agriculture Organization and the International Union for the Conservation of Nature. The English-man was Mr. Peter Hill, who from 1948 to 1951 was regional agronomist with the Overseas Food Corporation at Urambo in Tanganyika and since then has been working on farming projects in the Congo and Thane Riney. The two men began their tour in Senegal, and countries on their itinerary included Ethiopia, Mali, Ghana, Nigeria, Somalia, Sudan, Tanganyika, the Federa-tion of Rhodesia and Nyasaland and Bechuanaland. Their brief was to study African wild life in its natural habitat, to assess the extent of Africa's game resources, decide how they can best be developed, and advise African governments accordingly, and to help to train local people to carry out national programmes for resources development. This policy includes the conservation of wild life for tourist interest, for the production of protein food and for other scientific and cultural purposes.

Rupert Fothergill suggests the periodic interchange of wardens and other game officials between African countries.

With the conservation of great tracts of land tied to the fate of the game, ecology, which Chambers's Twentieth Century Dic-tionary defines as the study of animals, plants or peoples and institu-tions in relation to environment, is now increasingly—desperately —being put into practice by scientists, naturalists and adminis-trators and their co-workers, but time is short and money scarce.

Sir Richard Turnbull says that whether Africa's wild life and wild Nature can survive, or whether they will be destroyed, or whittled down to a bare remnant, will largely depend on the extent to which financial help can be provided by Europe and America.

The most important development of our time in saving the game has been the launching of the World Fund of which Prince Bernhard of the Netherlands is the President with the Duke of Edinburgh as President of the British Appeal. Both royal figures are staunch champions and protectors of wild animals. This international charity, founded by Nature-lovers and Nature experts and with headquarters in Zürich, Switzerland, has as its symbol the loveable Giant Panda which owes its survival to Man's protection. The Fund was given a great fillip when the London *Daily Mirror* in a special "Shock Issue" in October, 1961, of characteristically shattering punch devoted several pages of pictures and text to the plight of wild creatures, principally in Africa, and made a forceful appeal for contributions.

"Will YOU give a bob or two to help build the new 'Noah's Ark'?" the *Mirror*, which has the largest daily circulation in the world, asked its millions of readers. "The urgent need is for money—NOW. It takes cash to send in teams of experts to avert threatened disasters. It takes cash to make long-term conservation plans, to buy land for reserves, and to make the public aware of the danger. No matter what brilliance future generations may achieve in the realms of science and technology, they will never be able to make a dodo. Or any other wild creature that has become extinct.

"Man is in no way responsible for the drought which is killing thousands of animals all over the world today, but, by building dams and drilling waterholes, Man CAN do something to alleviate the dreadful sufferings of some of the wild beasts whose very existence he has threatened in so many short-sighted and wanton ways. For, quite apart from the neglect, the poaching and the hunting, Man is guilty of polluting rivers, lakes, even the sea . . . so bringing suffering and death to millions of birds, fish and other creatures.

"Guilty of spreading poisonous chemicals over millions of square miles of earth, thus killing thousands of birds which used to keep down the harmful insects that the poisons are designed to control.

"Guilty of vast engineering projects which take no account of the valuable wild life resources in the areas affected. . . .

"A state of emergency now exists for the wild life of the world. On current trends, several of the largest land animals may soon be exterminated.

"It is the responsibility of all who are alive today to accept the trusteeship of wild life, and to hand on to posterity as a source of wonder and interest, knowledge and enjoyment, the entire wealth of diverse animals and plants. This generation has no right by selfishness, wanton or unintentional destruction or neglect to rob future generations of this rich heritage.

Following the *Mirror's* strident call, 30,000 people in Britain alone subscribed £45,000 to the Fund, ranging from the £10,000 gift of a wealthy businessman to shilling postal orders and postage stamps from animal-loving old-age pensioners and children. Part of the total of these early gifts was used immediately to make urgent grants for protecting rhino in East Africa, and other monies were ear-marked for the early purchase of land to create another national park in Tanganyika. This project, and others similar, are typical of practical, vital uses to which the yawning coffers of the Fund are being put.

Africa's game, mankind's wealth of variety and beauty represented by a dwindling throng of the most varied and fantastic kinds of animal found anywhere on earth, face a total eclipse at the hands of Man. Wild life, part of the balance of Nature on which our existence depends, is a challenge to his self-respect.

Without whole-hearted, drastic and costly measures to meet the threat, the best that can be hoped for is that *something* may be preserved, and then, perhaps, only on a diminishing scale, in the next ten years or so.

Africa's unique creatures belong to the world, but too many

areas once abounding with big and small game are now either completely deserted or sustain only a few remnants of animals. Are the sweeping zoos without bars doomed to wither and die? Is Africa soon to cease to be an animals' paradise?

"Noah was commanded to build an ark and take into it a pair of every living creature to save them from the flood," said the Duke of Edinburgh at a banquet in New York organized to raise money for the World Wildlife Fund. "Today a different kind of deluge threaten's the earth's creatures and the World Wildlife Fund is the ark built by men, women and children throughout the world to give them a chance to survive the thoughtless actions of mankind."

The looming catastrophe is of a magnitude little comprehended abroad, or even in Africa itself.

I have endeavoured, as a result of a survey covering more than 30,000 miles, to show it as an overall picture of dark tragedy, inevitable in the matter of a few years unless, maybe, some form of interlocking campaign of salvation—a kind of continental "Operation Noah" supported by national and international agencies—is mounted and sustained, financially and otherwise, by sympathizers throughout the free world.

The World Wildlife Fund is showing the way ahead.

Yet meanwhile, across a land mass bigger than the United States, from the blue waters of Cape Town's Table Bay to the sandy moonscape of the Sahara, the great retreat of the harried, stricken animals goes on.

INDEX